Social Media Use in Chinese Export Sales

社交媒体在中国出口销售中的应用

周吉红 著

中国财富出版社有限公司

图书在版编目（CIP）数据

社交媒体在中国出口销售中的应用＝Social Media Use in Chinese Export Sales：英文 / 周吉红著 . —北京：中国财富出版社有限公司，2023.10

ISBN 978-7-5047-8005-8

Ⅰ.①社… Ⅱ.①周… Ⅲ.①传播媒介－应用－出口贸易－研究－中国－英文 Ⅳ.① F752.62

中国国家版本馆 CIP 数据核字（2023）第 208815 号

策划编辑	王桂敏	责任编辑	田　超　张天穹	版权编辑	李　洋
责任印制	梁　凡	责任校对	卓闪闪	责任发行	黄旭亮

出版发行	中国财富出版社有限公司		
社　　址	北京市丰台区南四环西路 188 号 5 区 20 楼	邮政编码	100070
电　　话	010-52227588 转 2098（发行部）	010-52227588 转 321（总编室）	
	010-52227566（24 小时读者服务）	010-52227588 转 305（质检部）	
网　　址	www.cfpress.com.cn	排　　版	北京伊帆信息技术有限公司
经　　销	新华书店	印　　刷	三河市悦鑫印务有限公司
书　　号	ISBN 978-7-5047-8005-8/F · 3740		
开　　本	710mm×1000mm　1/16	版　　次	2023 年 10 月第 1 版
印　　张	11	印　　次	2023 年 10 月第 1 次印刷
字　　数	203 千字	定　　价	78.00 元

版权所有·侵权必究·印装差错·负责调换

CONTRIBUTION OF SOCIAL MEDIA USE AND CULTURAL INTELLIGENCE OF SALESPERSON TO CUSTOMER-QUALIFICATION SKILLS, ADAPTIVE SELLING BEHAVIORS AND SALES PERFORMANCE: THE CASE OF EXPORT SALESPERSONS IN CHINA

Jihong Zhou

International College,

.... Major Advisor
(Assistant Professor Peerayuth Charoensukmongkol, Ph.D.)

The Examining Committee Approved This Dissertation Submitted in Partial Fulfillment of the Requirements for the Degree of Doctor of Philosophy (Management).

.... Committee Chairperson
(Chih_Cheng Fang, Ph.D.)

.... Committee
(Assistant Professor Peerayuth Charoensukmongkol, Ph.D.)

.... Committee
(Henzel Tagalog Embalzado, Ph.D.)

.... Dean
(Associate Professor Piboon Puriveth, Ph.D.)

ABSTRACT

Title of Dissertation	CONTRIBUTION OF SOCIAL MEDIA USE AND CULTURAL INTELLIGENCE OF SALESPERSON TO CUSTOMER-QUALIFICATION SKILLS, ADAPTIVE SELLING BEHAVIORS AND SALES PERFORMANCE: THE CASE OF EXPORT SALESPERSONS IN CHINA
Author	Jihong Zhou
Degree	Doctor of Philosophy (Management)
Year	2019

With the wide popularity of social media in business and life, there has been an increasing trend of social media use in sales in recent years. In international business, social media plays an important role in overcoming the time and space barriers between export salespeople and foreign buyers. However, due to the emergence of social media in about a decade, academic research about social media use in sales is lagging behind the practice. In particular, scarce research has explored the topic of international business. To fill this void, this study aimed to investigate whether and how export salespeople's social media use could contribute to sales performance. In addition, in view of the effectiveness of cultural intelligence in cross-cultural settings, this study regarded it as an important factor in the context of export selling via social media and aimed to examine its effectiveness in these non-face-to-face cross-cultural settings. The main objective of the study was to investigate the impact of social media use in sales and cultural intelligence on salesperson's outcome performance, and relationship performance. Drawing on adaptive selling theory, categorization theory, and Social Customer Relationship Management framework, this study proposed that adaptive selling behaviors and customer-qualification skills could be mediating factors that would explain the possible impact of social media use in sales and cultural intelligence on salesperson's outcome performance and relationship performance. In addition, this study explored the impact of cultural intelligence on customer-qualification skills and adaptive selling behaviors as well. This study adopted a questionnaire survey method to collect data from a sampling framework of 24191 export salespeople in China. 966 responses were usable for analysis. Results from the partial least square analysis showed that social media use in sales was positively associated with relationship performance, but this positive relationship was not statistically supported. Cultural intelligence was found to have a statistically supported positive association with the salesperson's outcome performance and relationship performance. Social media use in sales and cultural intelligence were found to be positively associated with customer-qualification skills and adaptive selling behaviors, which were statistically supported. In addition, the total effect analysis showed that customer-qualification skills and adaptive selling behaviors were significant factors which explained why export salespeople who used social media in sales and owned high cultural intelligence could reap good outcome performance and relationship performance. Research findings added to sales literature, social media literature, and cultural intelligence literature. In view of the research findings, it is recommended that export salespeople and sales organizations that aim to enhance the salesperson's performance in export selling via social media need to note that social media use alone is not sufficient to generate direct benefits for them. Salespeople need to integrate characteristics of social media in different sales processes to improve their customer-qualification skills and adaptive selling behaviors so that they can reap ideal sales performance. Meanwhile, sales organizations and salespeople also need to realize the importance of cultures of foreign customers particularly in cross-cultural selling. Therefore, they also need to develop the ability to understand and respond effectively in cross-cultural sales situations to enhance their chance to gain superior performance in export selling.

ACKNOWLEDGEMENTS

This research would not have been possible without the support of many people. First of all, I would like to express my sincere gratitude to my supervisor, Asst. Prof. Dr. Peerayuth Charoensukmongkol, who had offered professional and insightful comments for numerous revisions and kept encouraging and inspiring me during the whole process. Secondly, my gratitude goes to the committee members, Dr. Chih_Cheng Fang and Dr. Henzel Tagalog Embalzado, who offered valuable comments and suggestions. Thirdly, I would like to thank my family, in particular, my husband and my 72-year-old father-in-law for taking care of my two daughters and supporting me during my pursuit of the Ph.D. degree. I feel much indebted to my family who had experienced many difficulties in the last two years. Fourthly, I would like to thank those who made every endeavour to help me collect data, in particular, Ms. Jing Zhou, Mr. Liaoyuan Wen, and Mr. Ming Zhou as well as many of my friends and previous students, and those who participated in the survey and voluntarily provided suggestions and feedback about the research. Lastly, my gratitude goes to my friends and colleagues who keep encouraging and helping me all the time and two universities which are National Institute of Development Administration (NIDA), and Jingchu University of Technology for offering financial support.

Jihong Zhou

October 2019

TABLE OF CONTENTS

CHAPTER 1　INTRODUCTION ·· **001**

   1.1　Background ·· 001

      1.1.1　Social Media Use in Business ·· 001

      1.1.2　Social Media Use in Sales ·· 007

   1.2　Statement of Problems ·· 010

   1.3　Research Gaps ··· 011

   1.4　Research Objectives ·· 015

   1.5　Contribution of the Study ·· 018

      1.5.1　Academic Contribution ·· 018

      1.5.2　Practical Contribution ·· 019

CHAPTER 2　LITERATURE REVIEW ·· **020**

   2.1　Social Media Use in Sales ··· 020

      2.1.1　Definitions of Social Media Use in Sales ·· 024

      2.1.2　Factors Influencing Social Media Use in Sales ·· 024

      2.1.3　Outcomes of Social Media Use in Sales ·· 027

      2.1.4　Previous Research Contexts about Social Media Use in Sales ················· 030

2.2	Salesperson's Performance		038
2.3	Adaptive Selling Behaviors		041
	2.3.1	Definition of Adaptive Selling Behaviors	041
	2.3.2	Outcomes of Adaptive Selling Behaviors	042
	2.3.3	Antecedents of Adaptive Selling Behaviors	044
2.4	Salesperson's Customer-Qualification Skills		046
2.5	Cultural Intelligence(CQ)		048
2.6	Theories		053
	2.6.1	Adaptive Selling Theory	053
	2.6.2	Categorization Theory	058
	2.6.3	Social Customer Relationship Management Framework	061
2.7	Hypotheses Development		066
	2.7.1	Social Media Use in Sales and Salesperson's Customer-Qualification Skills	066
	2.7.2	Salesperson's Customer-Qualification Skills and Adaptive Selling Behaviors	067
	2.7.3	Social Media Use in Sales and Adaptive Selling Behaviors	068
	2.7.4	Adaptive Selling Behaviors and Salesperson's Performance	069
	2.7.5	Salesperson's Customer-Qualification Skills and Salesperson's Performance	070
	2.7.6	Social Media Use in Sales and Salesperson's Performance	071

  2.7.7 CQ and Salesperson's Customer-Qualification Skills ············ 073

  2.7.8 CQ and Adaptive Selling Behaviors ···································· 074

  2.7.9 CQ and Salesperson's Performance ··································· 075

CHAPTER 3 METHODOLOGY ··· **079**

 3.1 Research Context ··· 079

 3.2 Sample Selection ··· 080

 3.3 Data Collection Method ·· 083

 3.4 Questionnaire Development ·· 084

 3.5 Measurement ·· 085

  3.5.1 Social Media Use in Sales ··· 085

  3.5.2 Salesperson's Customer-Qualification Skills ·················· 086

  3.5.3 Adaptive Selling Behaviors ··· 086

  3.5.4 Salesperson's Performance ··· 086

  3.5.5 Cultural Intelligence ··· 088

 3.6 Control Variables ·· 089

  3.6.1 Gender ·· 089

  3.6.2 Age ·· 090

  3.6.3 Experience ··· 090

  3.6.4 Education ··· 091

  3.6.5 English Language Proficiency ··· 091

 3.7 Data Processing Tools and Analysis ··· 092

APPENDICES ··· **094**

    Appendix A   Questionnaire (English)··· 094

    Appendix B   Questionnaire (Chinese) ·· 106

BIBLIOGRAPHY ·· **117**

BIOGRAPHY ··· **162**

LIST OF TABLES

Table 2.1　Summary of Research Findings about Factors Influencing Social Media Use in Sales ··· 027

Table 2.2　Summary of Research Findings about Outcomes of Social Media Use in Sales ··· 029

Table 2.3　Summary of Research Contexts about Social Media Use in Sales ············ 032

Table 2.4　Summary of Research Hypotheses ··· 077

Table 3.1　Distribution of Export Salespeople in the Database in China's Top 20 Provinces and Municipalities by Export Value ····················· 082

LIST OF FIGURES

Figure 1.1　Most Famous Social Media Worldwide Ranked by the Number of Active Users ·· 002

Figure 2.1　ISTEA Sales Process Model (Adapted from Weitz [1978]) ····················· 042

Figure 2.2　The Simplified Chart of Adaptive Selling Framework (Adapted from Weitz, Sujan [1986]) ·· 057

Figure 2.3　IDIC Process of Managing Customer Relationship ······························ 062

Figure 2.4　The Conceptual Model ·· 078

Figure 3.1　Distribution of Export Salespeople in the Database by Trade Fields ········ 081

Figure 3.2　A Comparison of the Percentage of Export Value and that of Export Salespeople in the Database in China's Top 20 Provinces and Municipalities by Export Value ·· 083

CHAPTER 1   INTRODUCTION

1.1   Background

1.1.1   Social Media Use in Business

With the development of web2.0 technology, social media has become a mainstream communication tool in the world (Dolan et al., 2017; Nelson-Field & Taylor, 2012). More than 2/3 of the world's Internet population visits social media sites, spending nearly 10 percent of that time in virtual communities (Moore et al., 2015). At present, miscellaneous social media applications are available for users, e.g. Facebook, Instagram, Twitter, Weblog, Flickr, YouTube, LinkedIn, QQ, Line, etc. (Kaplan & Haenlein, 2010). Among them, Facebook enjoys the highest popularity in the world and has 2.27 billion active users as of January 2019, followed by YouTube with 1.90 billion active users and WhatsApp with 1.50 billion active users (Statista, 2019). Figure 1.1 presents the most famous social media worldwide ranked by the number of active users as of January 2019 (Statista, 2019).

It is interesting to note that WeChat, the most popular social media in China, ranks fifth by the number of active users in the world. However, it ranks first based on the number of monthly active users by country. According to WeChat (2019), the number of monthly WeChat active users (1.08 billion) is more than four times the number of Facebook monthly active users in India (0.26 billion), the country which has the largest Facebook monthly active users worldwide (Statista, 2019a). Moreover, Statista (2019b) indicated that while the number of monthly active social media users worldwide is expected to reach about 3.02 billion by 2021, 750 million of the users are expected to be particularly from China in 2022. These statistics suggest that China is and will remain to be the country with the largest number of monthly active social media users worldwide.

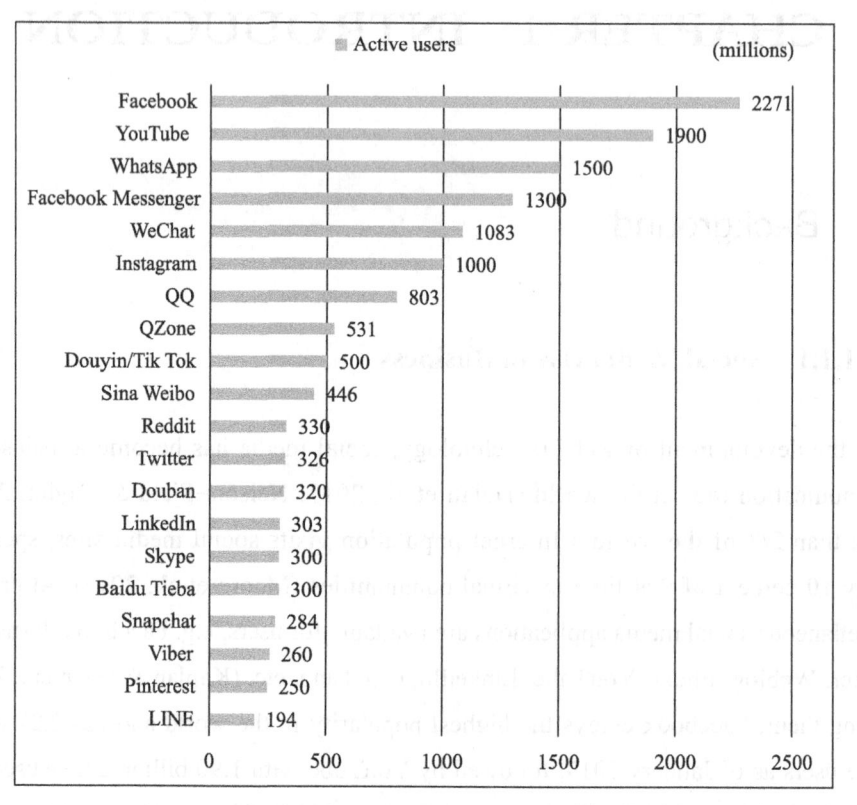

Social Media	Active users (millions)
Facebook	2271
YouTube	1900
WhatsApp	1500
Facebook Messenger	1300
WeChat	1083
Instagram	1000
QQ	803
QZone	531
Douyin/Tik Tok	500
Sina Weibo	446
Reddit	330
Twitter	326
Douban	320
LinkedIn	303
Skype	300
Baidu Tieba	300
Snapchat	284
Viber	260
Pinterest	250
LINE	194

Figure 1.1   Most Famous Social Media Worldwide Ranked by the Number of Active Users
Source: Statista, 2019

Attracted by the large population of social media users, business organizations have recognized the potential value of social media use and tried to harness its power for their benefit (Arnaboldi & Coget, 2016). It was reported that Fortune 100 companies maintained an average of 20 social media Web sites or accounts in the year 2010 (Rapp et al., 2013). IBM, one of the pioneering firms, had 76 micro-blog social media sites, 21 online video-sharing channels, and 80 employee blogs (Cox et al., 2008). They leverage the posted content and mutual conversation via social media to influence customer behaviors or forge stronger connections with customers(Rapp et al., 2013).

In general, firms are actively exploring the potential advantages of social media and leveraging it for various purposes such as marketing, internal and external relationship management, product innovation and branding, etc. (Alalwan, et al., 2017; Salo, 2017).

Firstly, marketing is one of the first and major area where business organizations utilize social media (Arnaboldi & Coget, 2016; Tarsakoo & Charoensukmongkol, 2019). In the white paper by Stelzner (2009), as many as 88% of surveyed marketers are using social media in their marketing. They conduct promotional campaigns on promising social media platforms with expectations to attract new customers (Michaelidou, et al., 2011), establish relationships with relevant stakeholders (Brennan & Croft, 2012), and communicate with targeted consumers (Gao & Feng, 2016; Harrigan et al., 2017; Kohli et al., 2015; Popp & Woratschek, 2016). Barnes et al. (2012) reported an increase in Fortune 500 companies' adoption of social media, such as blogs, Facebook and Twitter for marketing. Facebook's Annual Reports confirm that these companies are willing to spend a part of their budget on advertising through these main social media platforms (Falls, 2009). Facebook's 2016 Annual Report presented a 134.7% year-over-year increase in its advertising revenue from $1,974 million in 2010 to $17,928 million in 2015 (Facebook, 2016). Indeed, promotional activities conducted via social media could meet different marketing goals such as improving customer knowledge about products and services, awareness, perception, preferences, intention to buy, and actual purchase (Dehghani & Tumer, 2015; Duffett, 2015).

Secondly, businesses are taking full advantage of electronic word-of-mouth (e-WOM) interactive consumers create and distribute on social media platforms (Chu & Kim, 2011; Erkan & Evans, 2016; Teng et al., 2017). Social media is powerful in its social networking and information-sharing function (Erkan & Evans, 2016). So, the e-WOM posted on social media can go viral among the huge social media population and have great impacts on business organizations (Sohn, 2014). Obviously, businesses will benefit from positive e-WOMs posted on social media platforms. Ample anecdotal evidence has proved that positive e-WOMs on social media will lead to consumer purchase decisions. For instance, a study by Starcom MediaVest Group and Mashwork in 2012 found that 80% of surveyed IT decision-makers considered word-of-mouth as the most important source when making buying decisions and 58% of IT decision-makers use social media to learn from trustworthy peers (Maddox, 2013). A study by the ODM Group found that 74% of consumers rely on social media to guide purchase decisions (Beese, 2011). Another study reported that 43% of social media users purchase a product after sharing product information on Pinterest, Facebook or Twitter (Critical, 2013).

Thirdly, due to its great convenience in instant communication, businesses also use social media as an important tool for managing internal and external relationships (Alalwan et al., 2017; Arnaboldi & Coget, 2016; Jussila et al., 2014). Internally, social media offers a platform for employees to communicate with each other, disseminate information about management policies, and inform colleagues of the latest real-time movement about projects to facilitate the emotional communication between management and employees, strengthen collaboration among employees, and heighten employee loyalty and commitment (Arnaboldi & Coget, 2016). Externally, businesses utilize social media to establish and maintain relationships with customers and suppliers (Agnihotri et al., 2016; Alalwan et al., 2017; Rapp et al., 2011). By increasing the rate of content posting and sharing with customers over social media platforms, firms are more able to foster the level of interactivity and association with their customers, getting customers highly engaged with firms (Alalwan et al., 2017; Eagleman, 2013; Kaplan & Haenlein, 2010; Sanderson & Hambrick, 2012). Jussila et al. (2014) made a survey of 125 small and middle-sized enterprises (SMEs) operating in business-to-business (B2B) markets in Finland, finding that 30% of surveyed SMEs use social media and most of them use it for internal communication, and about 13% of them for customer/partner communication. Alalwan et al. (2017) reviewed 23 marketing researchers' academic papers, finding that 91% of these researchers strongly support organizations adopting social media as new tools to help sustain their relationship with targeted customers.

Fourthly, many business organizations make the best of social media for innovation-related purposes (B. Nguyen et al., 2015). Businesses can reach a large number of social media users for crowdsourcing by inviting them to participate in open innovation projects (Arnaboldi & Coget, 2016; Chesbrough, 2011) The number of ideas generated by participants will greatly increase the chances of success in hitting on a winning idea (Ogink & Dong, 2017). Moreover, following customers' advices shows businesses' respect to customers and concern about them, getting them highly engaged in product design and development and service improvement, in turn, beneficial to enhance customer satisfaction and improve customer loyalty and brand image(Leeflang, et al., 2014). As Scuotto, Del Giudice, Della Peruta, and Tarba (2017) pointed out, many companies (like Best Buy, Sears, Procter & Gamble, Adobe, BBC, BMW, Dell, LEGO, Salesforce, and Starbucks) have jumped on the bandwagon of using social media networks to improve their innovativeness. These companies have launched successful innovative campaigns or services such as Coca-Cola's 'Share a Coke' campaign, WeChat's 'red envelopes', and LEGO's new cocreation project entitled 'LEGO Ideas' (Ogink & Dong, 2017), and successfully gathered new innovative ideas through their dedicated online platform(Chesbrough, 2011). For firms, this open innovation tends to become cheaper, more efficient, and faster due to the use of digital social media platforms (Persaud, 2005). Possible valuable commercial outcomes together with lower cost and higher efficiency in such an open approach are driving more and more businesses to use social media for innovation purposes.

Fifthly, businesses use social media for branding purposes as well (Kohli et al., 2015; Michaelidou et al., 2011; Swani et al., 2017). As social media disseminates information faster and has the ability to amplify its effect, it provides an easier opening for new entrants to establish their brand identity and realize their brand recognition (Kohli et al., 2015). Moreover, social media allows information to be transmitted in various forms including texts, photos, and videos. The vividness of the transmitted information and powerful social networking lead to newer and innovative brands going viral quickly (de Vries et al., 2012). Besides that, firms utilize peer influence or powerful social networking to realize brand recognition and build consumer emotional bonds, as people tend to believe their peers' reviews or responses about a brand (Kohli et al., 2015). The dynamic two-way-communication interaction between firms and consumers on social media platforms is also beneficial to enhance consumer emotional bond with brands and enhance customers' loyalty to brands (Abeza et al., 2013; Michaelidou et al., 2011).

Facing the great influence of social media on branding, businesses act proactively by advertising on their own account pages on social media platforms, telling firm-generated brand stories to guide prospects to recognize their brands, interacting with consumers to strengthen their brand awareness and brand popularity(Swani et al., 2017) and even establishing brand communities for brand innovation(Gamboa & Goncalves, 2014; S. Singh & Sonnenburg, 2012). Zara, a pioneer among fast fashion companies, owns the largest number of and most valuable fans on Facebook. Customers have a large say in determining the brand's line: client suggestions are integrated into the clothes' production(Gamboa & Goncalves, 2014). As a result, fans of the Zara brand on Facebook were found to have a higher trust in the brand, perceived a higher value of Zara, and expressed more loyalty towards Zara, than those who did not follow Zara on Facebook (Gamboa & Goncalves, 2014).

Except for common purposes like marketing, relationship management, product innovation, and branding, different businesses take advantage of social media for their unique purposes as well. To name a few, some firms disclose corporate information, financial information such as annual report, earning releases, and other sensitive, market-moving news or events to the public on their social media account pages (Shilbury et al., 2003; Zhou et al., 2014). Other firms utilize the big data collected from social platforms as a source of information to obtain information from competitors, make predictions about market trends, targeted customers' consumption preferences, purchasing intention, and so on (Erkan & Evans, 2016; Hamilton et al., 2016; Patino et al., 2012; X. Wang et al., 2012; Zhu et al., 2016). Still others may use social media to identify potential candidates to be recruited (Arnaboldi & Coget, 2016).

To sum up, due to its wide popularity and great change in communication manner, social media has been widely used by companies of all sizes, in almost all industry sectors, for various purposes (Kaplan & Haenlein, 2010; Karimi & Naghibi, 2015; Rodriguez et al., 2013).

However, although social media has been applied in business for various purposes, one emerging trend of social media application in business is in the area of sales management (Nunan et al., 2018). As Nunan et al. (2018) have pointed out, there is a recent surge in research focusing on social media use in the sales fields. Research in this area mainly focuses on topics from the description of the status quo about social media use in sales to its impacting factors and outcomes (Agnihotri et al., 2016; Agnihotri et al., 2017; Agnihotri et al., 2012; Charoensukmongkol & Sasatanun, 2017; Itani et al., 2017; Lacoste, 2016; Moncrief et al., 2015; Ogilvie et al., 2018; Schultz et al., 2012). In spite of the soaring research about social media in sales, deeper research focusing on its working mechanism is still scarce and needs further exploration (Guesalaga, 2016; Lacoste, 2016).

1.1.2 Social Media Use in Sales

As mentioned above, social media is characterized with its huge social networking, interactivity, two-way communication, and 24-hour-7-day-a-week communication (Lacoste, 2016; Svatošová, 2012). In the sales industry, salespeople can leverage these characteristics and integrate social media into various sales processes such as prospecting, preapproaching, approaching, presentation, handling objections, closing a deal, and follow-up (Andzulis et al., 2012; Moore et al., 2015). Literature suggests that salespeople utilize social media for the following purposes.

Firstly, salespeople use wide social networks on social media to generate more sales opportunities (Järvinen & Taiminen, 2016; Okazaki & Taylor, 2013). According to Facebook, an average user has 130 friends on the social media (Hudson & Hudson, 2013); this means that salespeople have access to a large pool of prospects and referrals from customers or acquaintances through social media (Järvinen & Taiminen, 2016). Moore et al. (2015) reported that despite preferences in usage, both business-to-business (B2B) and business-to-consumer (B2C) sales professionals use social media in their selling and the most commonly used applications for social and professional networking are Facebook (45.4%) and LinkedIn (16.4%).

Secondly, as buyers often seek opinions from social networks or professional social media platforms, salespeople use social media to influence buyers' purchase intentions

(Agnihotri et al., 2012). According to Forrester Research, over 75% of 1200 surveyed business technology decision-makers utilize social media to obtain information or opinions on specific products and services (Ramos & Young, 2009). In a soft and gradual manner, salespeople influence buyers' purchase intentions by sharing links or responding to comments in their social media accounts, offering some solutions or suggestions, updating product information frequently via social media platforms, and even draw customers or prospects of interest into their own social networks (Agnihotri et al., 2012). The greater number of publications are posted, shared, and commented on social media, the greater influence salespeople have in social networks (Lacoste, 2016).

Thirdly, salespeople use social media to establish and maintain customer relationships (Andzulis et al., 2012; Charoensukmongkol & Sasatanun, 2017; Lacoste, 2016; Sasatanun & Charoensukmongkol, 2016). On one hand, sailes scholars regard social media as an ideal tool for relationship-oriented selling as its two-way communication feature allows salespeople to listen to their customers and make repeated interactions with them, which helps build trust and maintain customer relationship (Andzulis et al., 2012; Lacoste, 2016). On the other hand, as salespeople can obtain open information about customers' personal profiles on social media accounts, like their birthdays and preferences, salespeople have an opportunity to develop an interpersonal relationship with customers, for instance, sending greetings to customers on birthdays, festivals, or other special occasions (Agnihotri et al., 2012). Undoubtedly, a positive interpersonal relationship between seller and buyer complements and facilitates the development of business relationships(Lacoste, 2016).

Fourthly, salespeople use social media to reduce sales costs and enhance sales efficiency (Itani et al., 2017; Schultz et al., 2012) Salespeople can use social media to communicate with prospects or customers in a 24-hour-7-day-a-week manner, which, as a result, greatly reduces the frequency of face-to-face meetings and travel expenses (Itani et al., 2017; Schultz et al., 2012). For export sales, such an effect can be augmented due to the great geographic distance between exporters and importers (Bocconcelli et al., 2017). Moreover, a huge amount of free information available on some professional social media platforms such as LinkedIn and Facebook can potentially reduce sales organizations' investment in purchasing "cold call lists" from specialized vendors (Järvinen & Taiminen, 2016). In addition, unlike traditional prospecting processes during which salespeople adopt cold calling and canvassing to talk with unqualified prospects and waste a lot of time before they realize they are doing so (Lacoste, 2016), social media offer open information for salespeople to qualify leads early in the sales process, hence, salespeople can spend minimal time on less ideal customers but maximal time focusing on more promising opportunities, increasing salespeople's efficiency in the sales process (Alarcón-del-Amo et al., 2018; Moncrief & Marshall, 2005; Rodriguez et al., 2013; Trailer & Dickie, 2006).

From the perspective of sales management, businesses use social media to perform sales management tasks, such as supervision, training, recruiting, and so on (Moncrief et al., 2015; Rollins et al., 2014). More and better candidate information obtained from social media and convenience in virtual interviews will greatly improve recruiting efficiency and quality (Moncrief et al., 2015). Instant communication via social media reduces face-to-face periodic reporting times, which keeps sales managers informed of the real-time movement, making supervision easier (Moncrief et al., 2015). Social media also makes personalized training at the individual level possible (Rollins et al., 2014).

To sum up, while sales managers can utilize social media for their sales management, frontier salespeople are active in using social media as a sales channel and integrating it into every step of their sales process for more sales opportunities, more influences in buyers' purchasing behaviors, better customer relationship, less sales costs, and higher sales efficiency by taking advantage of characteristics of social media. However, despite the potential value of social media in sales, the actual use of social media by salespeople and sales organizations is not without problems (Guesalaga & Kapelianis, 2012; Nunan et al., 2018). Detailed delineation about problems in the current application of social media in sales is presented in the next part.

1.2　Statement of Problems

On one hand, due to social media's recent advent, its actual use in sales is still in an early period (Andzulis et al., 2012; Lacoste, 2016). Prior surveys show a low rate of actual adoption of social media in sales and both salespeople's and sales organizations' confusion about its role and value in sales (Durkin et al., 2013; Lacoste, 2016). According to Schultz and his colleagues (2012), 99% of business managers in their study believe that the use of social media will have a significant influence on their business but almost 2/3 of them claim that they are not sure of its meaning. The Sales Management Association in the U.S. found that 70% of the surveyed companies were either not using social media in sales, or just exploring its use(Guesalaga, 2016). The OgilvyOne global survey of salespeople found that only 9% of salespeople report any social media-related focus on sales by their own organizations (Featherstonehaugh, 2010). Many companies remain hesitant to leverage social media to assist sales (Agnihotri et al., 2012). For firms that haven't recognized social media as a professional tool, access may even be forbidden on firm premises (Lacoste, 2016).

On the other hand, academic studies report inconclusive findings about social media use in sales contexts. In terms of positive impacts, literature has found that social media use can serve as a selling tool, a helpful learning tool, and a sales training aid for salespeople and sales management (Mangold & Faulds, 2009; Marshall et al., 2012; Rollins et al., 2014). Social media use in sales can generate high-quality sales leads (Järvinen & Taiminen, 2016), help salespeople find business opportunities (Quinton & Wilson, 2016; Rodriguez et al., 2013), aid salespeople and firms in managing customer relationships (Moncrief et al., 2015; Moore et al., 2015; Rodriguez et al., 2013; Trainor, 2012; Trainor et al., 2014), enhance salespeople's responsiveness to customers' requests and information communication quality (Agnihotri et al., 2017; Hunter & Perreault Jr., 2007; Ogilvie et al., 2018; Rodriguez & Honeycutt Jr., 2011), as well as improve internal administrative performance and firm's sales performance (Hunter & Perreault Jr., 2007; Itani et al., 2017; Quinton & Wilson, 2016; Schultz et al., 2012; Trainor, 2012).

However, research also found some negative outcomes associated with social media use in sales like interruptions, tension, and work-life conflict that salespeople might experience when they use social media for sales activities (Gibbs et al.,2013; Ollier-Malaterre et al., 2013; Van Zoonen et al., 2017). For example, Marshall et al. (2012)'s qualitative research observed salespeople's negative sentiment about the impact of social media in their personal life and found that the 24-hour-7-day-a-week communication via social media demands individuals' more commitment and lengthened time to work, thereby causing interruptions in their personal life and work-life conflict. In terms of business performance, although scholars like Agnihotri et al. (2016), Schultz et al. (2012), and Trainor (2012) suggested that social media use in sales contributes to business performance, Rodriguez et al. (2013) found it bore no relationship with outcome sales performance, which is obviously contradictory with other scholars' findings. These inconclusive findings about social media use in sales in academic research cast doubt on whether and how social media can be integrated into sales for both individuals' and firms' benefits.

To conclude, both sales personnel and sales organizations have confusions about the role and value of social media use in sales. Prior inconclusive findings about its outcomes in academic fields may partially account for the relatively low rate of social media use in sales in practice and even compound such a situation. These practical and academic issues highlight the importance and necessity of more research on the topic. An investigation into the working mechanism of social media use in sales will provide insightful knowledge and recommendations for both sales organizations and salespeople.

1.3 Research Gaps

As social media has only become popular for about a decade, academic research is relatively lagging behind its wide popularity in practice (Nunan et al., 2018). The earliest research on social media in sales dates back to 2009 (Mangold & Faulds, 2009) and most of them are after 2010 (Andzulis et al., 2012; Charoensukmongkol, 2014; Dong & Wu, 2015; Levin et al., 2012; Rapp et al., 2013; Trainor et al., 2014), 6 years after Facebook coming into being with its active users reaching 500 million. The lagging academic research suggests some limited focus and interest in the study about social media and leaves great space for further exploration.

Literature suggests that the early scholars studying social media use in sales committed to identifying its value for salespeople and sales organizations (Mangold & Faulds, 2009; Marshall et al., 2012; Rollins et al., 2014). Some studies in this area also explored factors influencing salespeople and sales organizations' actual use of social media in sales (Alarcón-del-Amo et al., 2016; Alarcón-del-Amo et al., 2015; Groza et al., 2012; Itani et al., 2017; Moore et al., 2013; Schultz et al., 2012). Other scholars also proposed social media strategies for salespeople, sales managers, and sales organizations (Agnihotri et al., 2012; Andzulis et al., 2012; J. H. Kietzmann et al., 2011; Lacoste, 2016; Moncrief et al., 2015; Sood & Pattinson, 2012; Trainor, 2012). Recently, some research turns to investigate outcomes caused by salespeople and sales organizations' social media use in sales (Agnihotri et al., 2016; Agnihotri et al., 2017; Agnihotri et al., 2012; Charoensukmongkol & Sasatanun, 2017; Itani et al., 2017; Moncrief et al., 2015; Ogilvie et al., 2018; Schultz et al., 2012). Despite previous scholars' great contribution to research about social media use in sales, research focusing on the working mechanism of social media use in sales by sales force is still limited and warrants further exploration (Guesalaga, 2016; Lacoste, 2016).

In terms of the working mechanism of social media use in sales, previous scholars hold that the use of information technology alone is not enough to bring benefits for both salespeople and sales organizations; the effectiveness of information technology can be possible when it is utilized to improve salespeople's behaviors or skills first which inculdes presentation skills, targeting abilities, communication skills, and adaptive selling behaviors, etc. (Ahearne et al., 2008; Itani et al., 2017; Moncrief et al., 2015; Ogilvie et al., 2018). Among them, adaptive selling behavior draws much attention from scholars (Itani et al., 2017; Ogilvie et al., 2018). Adaptive selling behavior refers to salespeople's adjustments of sales behaviors according to their understanding of customers and selling encounters in the process of interacting with customers (Weitz et al., 1986). It is a crucial skill particularly in the selling situations when salespeople have to deal with various customer types and complex selling encounters (Weitz, 1981). Salespeople need to make adequate adjustments to satisfy different customers' needs so that they can achieve better sales performance (Weitz, 1981). Although scholars have identified the impact of salespeople's social media use in sales on their adaptive selling behaviors and sales performance in domestic selling contexts (Itani et al., 2017; Ogilvie et al., 2018), a limited number of studies have explored the impact of salespeople's social media use in an international selling context, particularly in the area of export sales (Alarcón-del-Amo et al., 2016; Alarcón-del-Amo et al., 2015; Bocconcelli et al., 2017). However, given that export salespeople tend to face more complex selling environments than domestic ones, whether the role of adaptive selling behavior in social media sales applies to export selling contexts remains a question and needs further empirical research to explore its role in this context (Itani et al., 2017). To address this research gap, this study will retest the impact of salespeople's social media use in sales on their adaptive selling behavior and their sales performance in the context of export selling via social media.

Further, facing a large number of social media users, how export salespeople can deal with the huge amount of information relevant to potential customers and make sure their work is efficient and productive is still a question (Agnihotri et al., 2012). In such a situation, salespeople may need to acquire some specific skills to cope with the complex information proceeding process to achieve better performance (Román & Iacobucci, 2010). The present study proposes that salespersons' customer-qualification skill is such a skill that may play a role in the effect of export salespeople's social media use in sales on salesperson performance. Customer-qualification skill is a kind of customer typology based on the human being's categorization ability. According to categorization theory, categorization is one of the most basic functions of all organisms, which reduces the complexity of the external stimulus world, improves the information processing efficiency, and offers more efficient and economical knowledge of things and people (J. Cohen & Basu, 1987). Scholars have found that salespeople's customer-qualification skills can help increase salespeople's effectiveness and efficiency in dealing with various customers in domestic selling contexts (Román & Iacobucci, 2010; Román & Rodríguez, 2015). Given its positive role in domestic selling contexts, this study argues that salesperson's customer-qualification skill might be an essential skill for export salespeople to deal with novel and diverse customers in exporting selling via social media. Still, the contribution of customer-qualification skills in the area of export selling through social media platforms is an issue that has not received solid clarification in research.

In addition, previous researchers on social media use in sales paid scarce attention to the role of salespeople's intercultural competency in the context of social media export selling. Export selling can be regarded as intercultural selling due to the cultural differences between export countries and import countries (Pandey & Charoensukmongkol, 2019). To achieve better performance in intercultural selling, salespeople may need to acquire some intercultural competency to help fulfill sales tasks (Charoensukmongkol, 2019b). However, the role of intercultural competency in the context of social media export selling is still a rarely discussed topic in research. Considering this research gap as well as the importance of intercultural competency of salesperson in international selling, this study argues that export salespeople's intercultural competency might play an important role in the quality of sales communication that salesperson make with foreign customers through social media. Although there are several conceptualizations of intercultural competence (K. Barker et al., 2017; Bauman & Shcherbina, 2018; Lieberman & Gamst, 2015; Matsumoto & Hwang, 2013), this study focuses on cultural intelligence (CQ). Literature shows CQ is an important capability necessary for everyone involved in cross-cultural settings(Ang et al., 2008). Extant research has proved that individuals with high CQ tend to perform effectively in face-to-face intercultural communication in sojourning countries or host countries (Ang & Van Dyne, 2015; Barakat et al., 2015; L.-Y. Lee & Sukoco, 2010; Suthatorn & Charoensukmongkol, 2018). Whether CQ can play a similar effective role in export selling via social media warrants further exploration. An investigation of whether CQ works in export selling via social media extends prior CQ research that did not investigate the role of CQ in computer-mediated communication, particularly in the context of social media communication.

Another gap in research about social media use in sales is in terms of countries where previous studies were conducted. At the present time, the majority of previous studies about social media use in sales are carried out in Western countries (Groza et al., 2012; Marshall et al., 2012; Michaelidou et al., 2011; Ogilvie et al., 2018; Rodriguez et al., 2013; Schultz et al., 2012; Trainor et al., 2014). There are limited studies on the salespersons' social media use in the Asian countries (Ainin et al., 2015; Charoensukmongkol & Sasatanun, 2017; Itani et al., 2017). Example studies in Asian countries can be Itani et al. (2017)'s research in India and Charoensukmongkol and Sasatanun (2017)'s research in Thailand. Itani et al. (2017) made an empirical study about the antecedents and outcomes of social media use in B2B sales in India. Charoensukmongkol and Sasatanun (2017) investigated the relationship between the intensity of social media use for customer relationship management and business performance satisfaction among Thai microenterprises. Despite these pioneering studies about social media use in sales in some Asian countries, more research about this topic in other Asian countries is still needed for a comprehensive understanding of salespeople's social media use in sales in distinctive Asian countries. This study targets on China, as it has the largest number of monthly active social media users in the world (Statista, 2019b). Moreover, as China implements an export-oriented economic development policy and has a large population of export salespeople, the country is supposed to have a huge number of export salespeople who use social media in sales. Therefore, China serves as a suitable context for the study of export salespeople' social media use in sales. An empirical study about Chinese export salespeople's social media use in sales will add to prior research conducted in other Asian countries and offer insightful knowledge for both academia and practitioners interested in knowing more about Asian export salespeople's social media selling behaviors.

1.4 Research Objectives

The objective of this research is not only to fill the research gaps mentioned earlier, but also to provide extra evidence to support the issues that are unclear or inconclusive in previous research. The main objective of the present study is to explore the impact of export salesperson's social media use in sales on salesperson's performance. This research also examines the mediating factors that explain the possible linkage between social media use in sales and salesperson's performance. Regarding the mediating variables, this study proposes that adaptive selling behaviors and salesperson's customer-qualification skills might explain why social media use in sales can be linked to salesperson's performance. Further, this study examines the impact of CQ on salesperson's customer-qualification skills, adaptive selling behaviors, and salesperson's performance as well.

This study uses three theories as its theoretical support for hypothesis development. First, this research adopts the Adaptive Selling Theory as the main theoretical support to explain the pathway of the effect of export salesperson's social media use, their adaptive selling behaviors, customer-qualification skills and CQ on their performance. According to the Adaptive Selling Theory proposed by Weitz et al. (1986), the characteristics of a salesperson like his capabilities can influence his motivation and behavior to practice adaptive selling, which, in turn, facilitates sales performance. The theory argues that when salespeople adapt their sales approaches in personal selling to fit the perceptions of customers, their successful adjustments will improve sales performance. In addition, the effectiveness of a salesperson's adaptive selling behavior depends on his capabilities. A salesperson's capabilities are composed of such abilities as knowledge dimensions and such skills as information collection skills. For instance, they argue that as a capacity of salespeople, information collection skill is critical for salespeople to practice adaptive selling effectively, because a salesperson needs an elaborate knowledge structure about customers and selling environments in order to make adequate adjustments during interactions (Weitz et al., 1986). Given this, this study regards social media use in sales as salespeople's information collection skill in that social media offers a channel for salespeople to collect information about foreign customers (Lacoste, 2016). The collected information then forms a basic knowledge structure required to practice adaptive selling behavior. Following the main argument of this theory, this study argues that social media use in sales is conducive to adaptive selling behavior, which in turn improves salespeople's performance. Further, as customer-qualification skill reflects a salesperson's refined knowledge structure about customers (Román & Iacobucci, 2010), this study argues that it can be regarded as a salespeople's capability to practice adaptive selling behaviors as well. In a similar fashion, given CQ itself signifies a person's knowledge structure about different cultures necessary to practice adaptive selling behaviors in cross-cultural settings (Hansen et al., 2011), this study holds that it meets with the knowledge dimension of salespeople's capabilities to practice adaptive selling behaviors to satisfy cultural preferences of foreign customers too. All in all, following the main arguments of the Adaptive Selling Theory, this study proposes that social media use, salespeople's customer-qualification abilities, and CQ are components of salespeople's capabilities and all three factors contribute to salespeople's performance by improving their adaptive selling behaviors.

Second, this study uses categorization theory to support the mediating role of customer-qualification skills in explaining the contribution of social media use in sales and CQ to adaptive selling behaviors and salespeople's performance. According to categorization theory, people classify things and persons in groups for more efficient and economical knowledge (Cantor & Mischel, 1979). So, categorization reduces people's cognitive burden in information processing and improves effectiveness and efficiency in various cognitive activities (Bruner et al., 1956). Salespeople's customer-qualification skill, which is a customer typology based on categorization, is consistent with the categorization theory. The reasons for the consistency are twofold. Firstly, because salespeople's customer-qualification skills allow export salespeople to have a refined knowledge structure about customers, they are beneficial to practicing adaptive selling behaviors (Román & Iacobucci, 2010); Secondly, because customer-qualification skills reduce complexity in proceeding huge amount of information on social media, they improve salespeople's effectiveness and efficiency in information processing (Román & Iacobucci, 2010). These two contributions of customer-qualification skills imply that it can mediate the contribution of social media use in sales and CQ to adaptive selling behaviors and salespeople's performance.

Third, this study uses social customer relationship management (CRM) theoretical framework to explain the impact of social media on customer-qualification skills and adaptive selling behaviors, which in turn contribute to relationship performance. Social CRM argues that the integration of social media into customer-facing activities can engage customers in collaborative conversations and improve customer relationships (Trainor, 2012). According to social CRM, firms need to engage in a four-step IDIC process (Identification, Differentiation, Interaction, and Customization) to achieve optimal customer relationship performance (Trainor et al., 2014). In the Identification step, firms collect customer information available on social media to identify customers' needs and values. Then, in the Differentiation step, firms classify customers into different groups according to identified customer needs and values. In the Interaction step, firms make multiple interactions with customers for a further understanding of the details of customer needs and behaviors. In the customization process, firms make adaptations to selling behaviors to offer customized solutions to meet customer needs and expectations. Social CRM has been mostly used to explain firms' CRM strategy, but recent scholars argue that it is applicable to salesforces' selling behaviors as well (Peppers & Rogers, 2016). This study keeps in alignment with previous scholars to regard salespeople's selling activities as customer-facing activities and draws on this theory to explain the impact of social media use on customer-qualification skills and adaptive selling behaviors, which in turn lead to optimal relationship performance. This study argues that the four steps of IDIC match well with customer-qualification skills and adaptive selling behaviors. To be specific, the Identification and Differentiation steps of the IDIC process involve customer-qualification skills, and the Interaction and Customization steps of the IDIC process reflect the process of adaptive selling behaviors. Therefore, following the social CRM framework, this study proposes that social media use in sales will first contribute to customer-qualification skills and adaptive selling behaviors, resulting in a success in customer relationship performance.

1.5 Contribution of the Study

1.5.1 Academic Contribution

This study will contribute to the current literature from two aspects. Firstly, this study will contribute to the existing literature about social media use in export selling contexts.

Given the new emergence of social media, scarce empirical research offers direct evidence about whether export salespersons' social media use contributes to their sales performance and explores deeply its working mechanism. The present research findings will help uncover the possible mediating variables that might explain the contribution of export salespeople's social media use to their sales performance.

Secondly, this study will add to the current CQ literature by exploring the role of CQ in non-face-to-face communication, particularly in social media export selling. Given that little research has identified the important role of CQ in non-face-to-face intercultural communication, the results from this research regarding the role of CQ in social media communication will clarify whether CQ tends to matter in this communication context. This study's findings will offer empirical evidence to explain the possible contribution of CQ to export salespeople's selling skills, behaviors, and performances in the context of social media export selling.

1.5.2 Practical Contribution

This study will offer insights for export sales managers and practitioners. As discussed earlier, sales managers and organizations are hesitant to embrace social media in the workplace due to their failure in recognizing the potential benefits of social media use in sales and their lack of understanding of the working mechanism of social media use in sales. This study's findings are expected to offer empirical evidence from Chinese export industry and clarify how social media use in sales can contribute to salespeople's performance. Export sales managers and their sales representatives will have a better understanding about what capabilities, competencies, skills, and behaviors are needed for salespeople to improve their sales performance and generate more revenue for companies in social media exporting contexts.

CHAPTER 2 LITERATURE REVIEW

This chapter will first review the literature involving the main variables in this research which are social media use in sales, salesperson performance, adaptive selling behavior, salesperson's customer-qualification skills, and culture intelligence. Then, the author will introduce key theories that offer theoretical support for hypothesis development. The final part of this chapter presents the hypothesis proposed in this research.

2.1 Social Media Use in Sales

In general, due to its great access to wide social networks and convenience in mutual interactions between users, social media has been widely used in business for marketing, customer relationship management, product innovation, branding, etc. (Rapp, et al., 2011; Salo, 2017). In sales, both companies and sales personnel find utility in social media use as well(Moore et al., 2015). Prior literature has identified and documented the important role of social media use in sales (Bocconcelli et al., 2017; Mangold & Faulds, 2009; Marshall et al., 2012; Rollins et al., 2014). For instance, Mangold and Faulds (2009) are among the first researchers to point out the vital role of social media in marketing and sales, arguing that social media should be a hybrid element of a firm's promotion mix. Later, Marshall et al. (2012)'s research identified social media as a generational and global sales interface, bringing great connectivity for salespeople and customers, and a dominant selling tool bringing a revolution in buyer-seller relationship. Rollins et al. (2014) also observed that social media can be a helpful learning tool for salespeople and companies. In addition, Bocconcelli et al. (2017)'s research proposed that social media represents an innovative resource in SMEs' sales process with regard to first contact and communication activities, and a strategic resource to implement an effective business networking effort.

Realizing the important role of social media use in sales, salespeople and companies try to experiment with various practices and strategies to leverage them in sales activities (Itani et al., 2017; Schultz et al., 2012). Sales researchers not only depicted the status quo of social media use in sales (Moore et al., 2015; Swani et al., 2014), but also provided theoretically suggested strategies for sales managers and companies to follow (Andzulis et al., 2012; J. H. Kietzmann et al., 2011; Lacoste, 2016; Sood & Pattinson, 2012; Trainor, 2012). Researchers find that companies and salespeople use social media with different preferences or in various ways (Swani et al., 2014; Swani et al., 2017). For instance, by comparing B2B and B2C salespeople's social media use in the selling process, Moore et al. (2013)'s research shows that B2B salespeople tend to use social media targeted at professionals whereas their B2C counterparts tend to utilize more social media sites targeted to the general public for engaging in one-on-one dialogue with their customers. They also find that B2B professionals tend to use relationship-oriented social media technologies more than B2C professionals for the purpose of prospecting, handling objections, and after-sale follow-up. Moreover, Swani et al. (2014) also showed that Fortune 500 companies posted more messages about direct calls to purchase in B2C tweets than in B2B ones.

Theoretically, researchers drew on varied theories and proposed a series of strategies for sales professionals and organizations regarding the use of social media (Agnihotri et al., 2012; Sood & Pattinson, 2012; Trainor, 2012). For instance, Agnihotri, Kothandaraman, Kashyap, and Singh (2013) adopted task-technology fit theory as their theoretical support to propose a social media strategy framework for B2B organizations to increase customer engagement and create customer value. The authors argue that when salespeople's service behaviors fit social media use, the fit creates value for both customers and salespeople. A set of detailed social media strategies about goal delineation, information exchange, competitive intelligence, and performance metrics are proposed for B2B salespeople and organizations to improve service behaviors and create value in the process of social media use in sales. With respect to CRM, Trainor

(2012) recommended that companies should integrate social media technology into it to benefit business performance. In Sood and Pattinson (2012)'s research, the authors build on the traditional industrial marketing and purchasing (IMP) interaction model to propose a new IMP interaction model for contemporary B2B sales and marketing interactions. The original IMP interaction model emphasizes the importance of human-to-human interaction for B2B selling and marketing activities. The authors argue that since human-to-human interaction is the heart of social media interaction, social media can be integrated into key thought processes of IMP. In the new IMP social framework, product/service exchange, information exchange, financial exchange, and social exchange via various social media all contribute to cooperation and adaptations (Sood & Pattinson, 2012).

In light of Walker, Churchill, and Ford (1979)'s sales management model, Moncrief et al. (2015) examined the impact of social media on sales management from two major aspects: sales management functions (supervision, training, selection, compensation, and deployment) and salesperson performance (role, aptitude/skill, and motivation). Their research offered some suggestions to help sales managers and salespersons better adapt to the post-social media sales environment. For instance, when sales managers are fulfilling their training functions, a common practice in pre-social media training is to ask a new salesperson to observe a more experienced salesperson or sales manager on the job. In contrast, the post-social media training can be implemented through packaged online programming via social media which is customized to meet the needs of each new hire and allows the trainee to learn at home at his own pace. The impact of social media on sales management is that training becomes personalized at the individual level. To cope with this change, the authors recommended that the sales managers should "recalibrate the menu of training options to meet the learning preferences of a new generation of salespeople" (Moncrief et al., 2015).

Unlike the above scholars' heavy reliance on borrowing existing theories to propose social media strategies (Agnihotri et al., 2012; Sood & Pattinson, 2012; Trainor, 2012), other scholars establish social media strategies by digging into features of social media communication and integrating these features into sales processes and activities (Andzulis et al., 2012; T. C. Kietzmann et al., 2011). Among the pioneering proponents for social media use in sales, Andzulis et al. (2012) proposed detailed social media strategies applicable for salesforce in each step of the sales process which includes understanding the customer, approaching the customer, needs discovery, presentation, close, service, and follow-up. For instance, at the step of approaching customers, sales forces are advised to use social media to establish credibility by launching Facebook promotions to invite participation in new product testing. At the stage of needs discovery, salespeople are advised to ask their Facebook fans to vote in polls or comment on proposed changes to products, services, or logos. In this way, salespeople can better understand customers' needs and buying motives.

For sales organizations, J. H. Kietzmann et al. (2011) provided a framework to define social media by seven building blocks (identity, conversations, sharing, presence, relationships, reputation, and groups) and offered suggestions for firms about how to develop strategies to monitor, understand, and respond to different social media activities in each block. Lacoste (2016) modified J. H. Kietzmann et al. (2011)'s framework by interweaving virtual relationships via social media into traditional physical relationships and proposed a model for key account managers to use social media in their customer relationship management. Lacoste (2016)'s model consists of five building blocks which are identity (use social media to unveil professional identity), reputation/credibility (use social media to create "personal" value), connection (use social media to connect to potential key account customers), retention (use social media to increase customer retention), and engagement (deepen customer engagement by switching from virtual communication to face-to-face relationships). In comparison with Andzulis et al. (2012)'s and J. H. Kietzmann et al. (2011)'s strategies, Lacoste (2016)'s model is more suitable for selling to and managing key account customers. This development suggests that studies focusing on social media use in sales shift from the general sales environment to more specific and nuanced sales contexts.

To date, apart from the depiction of the status quo of social media use in sales, the identification of its importance, and the theoretically conceptualized strategies for sales professionals and organizations, recent researchers have committed more efforts to explore why sales professionals and organizations show different patterns of social media use in sales, as well as what motivates them to adopt social media in sales activities and what are the impacts of social media use in sales (Agnihotri et al., 2012; Itani et al., 2017; Nunan et al., 2018; Ogilvie et al., 2018; Sasatanun & Charoensukmongkol, 2016). In view of this, the following parts will review the literature about social media use in sales from four aspects in the following sequence. First, the next section will begin by providing the definition of social media in sales. Then, a review of the literature about factors influencing social media in sales and its outcomes will be provided. The final part will make a conclusion about research contexts in previous research, to further highlight possible research gaps and to pinpoint the research scope of this study.

2.1.1 Definitions of Social Media Use in Sales

Social media use in sales is defined as " the intensity with which social media is used in a company's sales organization, considering social media as web-based applications including LinkedIn, Twitter, Facebook, YouTube, Google+, and similar media that foster social interaction" (Guesalaga, 2016). Besides, it is defined as a salesperson's utilization and integration of social media technology to perform his or her job (Agnihotri et al., 2012). Guesalaga (2016)'s definition stresses the use of social media by sales organizations and the frequency of social media use for the purpose of social interaction at the firm level. In comparison, Agnihotri et al. (2012)'s definition focuses on salespeople's application of social media and the integration of social media in their jobs. Overall, these definitions of social media use in sales provided in prior studies are used to formulate the definition of social media use in export activities of salespeople for this research. In this study, social media use in sales refers to a salesperson's use of social media for exporting sales of goods and services in his daily sales process. This definition narrows the scope of sales activities down and limits it within export sales activities.

2.1.2 Factors Influencing Social Media Use in Sales

Researchers analyzed various factors influencing salespeople's and organizations' adoption of social media in sales (Alarcón-del-Amo et al., 2016; Alarcón-del-Amo et al., 2015; Guesalaga, 2016; Itani et al., 2017; Levin et al., 2012; Rapp, et al., 2011). Regarding the personal characteristics of salespeople, Levin et al. (2012) found three factors that motivate salespersons to use social media for their sales activities, namely apathetic motivation, extrinsic motivation, and intrinsic motivation. The three motivations together with voluntariness and past performance influence new sales employees' participation in adopting social media. Itani et al. (2017) note that learning goal orientation plays a significant role in explaining salespeople's attitudes towards social media; they also acknowledge that salespeople who have more positive attitudes about social media tend to have more actual social media use. Moreover, the authors found that for individuals with a high level of learning goal orientation, such a positive effect tends to be stronger. In terms of CRM, Moore et al. (2015) coined a new term social CRM and defined it as the activity of salespeople using relationship-oriented social media to accomplish job-related and selling processes. They observed that the frequency and extent of social CRM depend on the specific social media tools used and the stage of the selling process. In particular, B2B sales managers are found to be significantly and far more engaged with social CRM than sales representatives. Interestingly, Schultz et al. (2012) found that age and social media norms are factors influencing salespeople's social media usage as well. They found that younger salespeople are more likely to use social media, and salespeople tend to use social media more when social media norms reflect its usage by supervisors, customers, competitors, and colleagues. In addition, Wang, Hsiao, Yang, and Hajli (2016) found that in an online community context (LinkedIn), sellers' social identity and social comparison are key factors motivating them to develop a series of co-innovation activities with customers in online communities.

Regarding the factors motivating the organizations to use social media in sales activities, Groza et al. (2012)'s research found that the degree of cross-departmental cooperation within a firm positively contributes to its sales force's social media use. Rapp, et al. (2013) draw on the Contagion theory to investigate the contagion effect of social media use across suppliers, sellers, and customers. The Contagion theory holds that people's behaviors, similar to a disease, are transmittable and may change after an interaction with another person or group. Their research findings prove that supplier salesperson's social media use positively influences retailer social media use and in turn customer social media use. Similarly, Guesalaga (2016) proposed two individual factors (sales manager's competence and commitment to social media), two organization factors (supplier company's competence and commitment to social media), and one customer factor (buying companies' engagement with social media) as antecedents of sales organizations' social media use in sales. Their research findings offered empirical evidence to support all the proposed factors but one individual factor (individual commitment to social media) as antecedents of sales organizations' social media use in sales. In addition, Alarcón-del-Amo et al. (2015) used the resource-based view (RBV) to explore the effect of export companies' social media competence (SMC) on their actual social media use and business performance. According to the RBV theory, when a firm adopts strategies based on its strategic resources and capabilities, it will achieve superior firm performance and a sustainable competitive advantage (Barney, 1991). Based on this theory, Alarcón-del-Amo et al. (2015) regarded social media as an export company's technological resource and defined SMC as a company's potential in applying social media to perform communication activities and effectively manage information about companies and customers. They investigated its role in determining export companies' actual use of social media and found that export companies' SMC influences their actual social media use indirectly via their intention to use it (Alarcón-del-Amo et al., 2015).

To sum up, salespeople's individual characteristics like age and social identity, their motivations, voluntariness, past performance, attitudes, and beliefs towards social media are mostly identified as the main factors influencing their social media use (Itani et al., 2017; Levin et al., 2012; Schultz et al., 2012; Y. Wang et al., 2016). For firms, the management's attitudes and beliefs towards social media, companies' competence relevant to social media, supplier and customer companies' social media use, and cross-departmental cooperation predict the actual adoption of social media by companies (Alarcón-del-Amo et al., 2016; Alarcón-del-Amo et al., 2015; Groza et al., 2012; Guesalaga, 2016; Rapp, et al., 2011). A summary of factors influencing salespeople's and companies' social media use in sales is presented in Table 2.1.

Table 2.1 Summary of Research Findings about Factors Influencing Social Media Use in Sales

Level	Authors	Findings
Individual level	Levin et al. (2012)	Motivations, voluntariness, and past performance influence new sales employees' participation in social media use
	Schultz et al. (2012)	Age negatively affects social media usage, while social media norms positively affect it. The younger a salesperson is, the more likely he will use social media in sales. A salesperson's customers, competitors, peer salespeople, and supervisors' social media use have an influence on his adoption as well
	Moore et al. (2015)	B2B managers are significantly and far more engaged with social CRM than sales representatives. The frequency and extent of social CRM usage vary based on the specific tools used and the stage of the selling process
	Y. Wang et al. (2016)	Sellers' social identity and social comparison are key factors motivating them to develop a series of co-innovation activities in an online community context (LinkedIn)
	Itani et al. (2017)	A salesperson's goal orientation and attitude toward social media interact to positively influence social media use. A salesperson's attitudes toward social media usefulness, as well as a salesperson's learning orientation, will influence how much a salesperson uses social media to assist in day-to-day job tasks
Firm level	Groza et al. (2012)	Social media use among the sales force is greater within firms that have a high degree of cross-departmental cooperation
	Rapp, et al. (2013)	The effect of supplier social media usage on retailer social media usage and in turn on customer social media usage is moderated by brand reputation and service ambidexterity
	Alarcón-del-Amo et al. (2015)	Social media competency (SMC) has an influence on the firm's actual use of these social media applications, which in turn has an impact on the firm's performance. The intention to use social media applications mediates the relationship between the firm's SMC and its social media usage
	Alarcón-del-Amo et al. (2016)	Managers' beliefs about social media capabilities for dealing with foreign customers directly influence managerial attitudes toward and intention to use social media, and also indirectly on the intention to use them through the attitude
	Guesalaga (2016)	Organizational competence and commitment to social media are key determinants of social media usage in sales, as well as individual commitment to it. Customer engagement with social media also predicts social media usage in sales, both directly and (mostly) through the individual and organizational factors analyzed, especially organizational competence and commitment

2.1.3 Outcomes of Social Media Use in Sales

Literature shows that social media use in sales can improve a firm's sales capabilities and various business performances (Groza et al., 2012; Quinton & Wilson, 2016; Rodriguez et al., 2013). For instance, Rodriguez et al. (2013)'s research reported that a selling organization's social media use improves its ability to create more opportunities, to understand customers, and to manage customer relationships in sales processes more effectively. With respect to business performance, social media use in sales has been found to improve a firm's sales performance (Groza et al., 2012; Quinton & Wilson, 2016), relationship performance (Quinton & Wilson, 2016; Rodriguez et al., 2013), as well as brand performance, retailer performance, and consumer-retailer loyalty(Rapp, Beitelspacher, et al., 2013).

In addition, scholars have investigated more detailed pathways about the impact of social media use on business performance. For instance, Wang, Pauleen, Zhang (2016)'s research stated that SMEs' social media use in sales enhances business performance in terms of marketing, innovation, and collaboration via improved communication performance. Ogilvie et al. (2018)'s recent research concluded that salespeople's social media use in sales contributed to their firms' customer relationship performance and objective sales performance through salespeople's enhanced communication and adaptability behaviors.

Regarding the outcomes that salespersons achieved from social media use in sales, literature shows that a major direct outcome is an improvement in salespeople's behaviors (Agnihotri et al., 2016; Agnihotri et al., 2012; Itani et al., 2017; Ogilvie et al., 2018). According to prior researchers' findings, salespeople's social media use can improve their service behaviors (Agnihotri et al., 2017; Agnihotri et al., 2012), information communication behaviors(Agnihotri et al., 2016; Ogilvie et al., 2018), adaptability behaviors (Ogilvie et al., 2018), and collection of competitive intelligence (Itani et al., 2017). In addition, salespeople's social media use has also been found to enhance their responsiveness to customers' needs and requests and customers' satisfaction with them by improved information communication (Agnihotri et al., 2016).

With respect to salespeople's sales performance, scholars find that salespeople who use social media in sales tend to indicate higher sales outcome performance than those nonusers (Schultz et al., 2012), and those users with high frequency of social media use tend to report higher satisfaction with their business performance than those with low frequency (Charoensukmongkol & Sasatanun, 2017). Itani et al. (2017)'s research also found that salespeople's social media use in their daily job tasks can contribute to their sales performance by improving their competitive intelligence and adaptive selling behavior.

To conclude, the current literature has documented the positive impacts of social media use in sales on a wide array of salespeople's behaviors and sales performance (Lacoste, 2016; Nunan et al., 2018). Prior researchers have proved that social media use can help generate high-quality sales leads, enhance a firm's sales abilities, and improve various business performances (Agnihotri et al., 2017; Agnihotri et al., 2012; Lacoste, 2016; Nunan et al., 2018; Ogilvie et al., 2018). A summary of research findings about outcomes of social media use in sales is presented in Table 2.2.

Table 2.2 Summary of Research Findings about Outcomes of Social Media Use in Sales

Level	Authors	Findings
Individual level	Agnihotri et al. (2012)	Salespeople's social media use can have a positive influence on service behaviors that influence value creation for customers as well as for salespeople
	Schultz et al. (2012)	Salespeople who use social media tend to indicate higher sales outcome performance than those nonusers
	Moncrief et al. (2015)	Social media is changing the role of sales managers and sales management functions. Eight lessons are presented for each sales manager to embrace
	Agnihotri et al. (2016)	Salespeople's social media use is an antecedent of enhancing their behaviors to increase customer satisfaction. Their social media use is found to enhance information communication behaviors, which improve salespeople's responsiveness and customer satisfaction
	Agnihotri et al. (2017)	Salespeople using CRM technology in conjunction with social media are more likely to exhibit higher levels of salesperson service behaviors than their counterparts with low social media technology use
	Charoensukmongkol and Sasatanun (2017)	Entrepreneurs who used social media intensively for CRM tended to report higher satisfaction with their business performance
	Itani et al. (2017)	Salespeople's social media use contributes to the improved collection of competitive intelligence as well as more adaptive selling behaviors, both of which lead to an increase in sales performance
	Ogilvie et al. (2018)	Salespeople's social media technology use enhances their communication and adaptability behaviors

Continued

Level	Authors	Findings
Firm level	Rodriguez et al. (2013)	B2B selling organizations' social media usage has a positive relationship with their ability to create sales opportunities and manage relationships. In terms of performance, the study found that social media usage has a positive relationship with relationship sales performance, but not outcome-based sales performance
	Groza et al. (2012)	Sales force's social media use contributes to the firm's sales performance and the effect is enhanced by developmental training in the organization
	Rapp, et al. (2013)	A selling organization's social media use positively contributes to its brand performance, retailer performance, and consumer–retailer loyalty
	Trainor et al. (2014)	The research finds that a firm's social media technology use, when viewed as a resource, improves its social CRM capabilities, which positively influences customer relationship performance
	Quinton and Wilson (2016)	The use of a particular professional social media platform LinkedIn helps develop business relationships and enhance business performance
	Järvinen and Taiminen (2016)	The use of marketing automation (involving social media use) in the B2B selling process generates high-quality sales leads through behavioral targeting and content personalization
	W. Y. C. Wang et al. (2016)	SMEs' social media use enhances their business performance in terms of marketing, innovation, and collaboration through improved communication performance
	Y. Wang et al. (2016)	Sellers' co-innovation with customers in online communities (LinkedIn) improves their companies' brand performance
	Ogilvie et al. (2018)	Salespeople's social media technology use enhances their communication and adaptability behaviors, which contributes to the firm's customer relationship performance and objective sales performance

2.1.4 Previous Research Contexts about Social Media Use in Sales

Although prior studies have identified the important role, factors, and outcomes of social media use in sales at both salespeople's individual level and companies' organizational level, social media use in different sales contexts has not been fully explored due to the advent of social media in recent years (Itani et al., 2017; Nunan et al., 2018; Salo, 2017). This study made a detailed analysis of research contexts in previous studies about social media use in sales. The analysis not only depicts the status quo of sales contexts scholars are mainly concerned about and have explored, but also reveals possible research gaps for future research about the topic.

From the in-depth review of the literature on social media use in sales from 2004 (the year Facebook was established) to the present, the author identified thirty relevant research articles on social media use in sales. Excluding conceptual research papers, the author finally got twenty-four empirical research papers. On the basis of sample and data information, these papers are grouped into three research contexts in which social media are used in sales activities including domestic sales, international sales, and both domestic and international sales. Findings regarding current research contexts about social media in sales are presented as follows.

Of all the twenty-four empirical papers, eighteen papers are conducted in domestic sales contexts (e.g. Lacoste, 2016; Levin et al., 2012; Schultz et al., 2012), four papers cover both domestic and international sales business (Agnihotri et al., 2017; Charoensukmongkol & Sasatanun, 2017; Itani et al., 2017; Lacoste, 2016), and two papers only focus on export selling (Alarcón-del-Amo et al., 2016; Alarcón-del-Amo et al., 2015). These statistics show that the majority of empirical researches about social media use in sales focus on domestic sales contexts and less attention is paid to international sales contexts.

In addition, studies on social media use in sales activities in the area of domestic sales contexts are conducted in a few countries such as the U.S., U.K., France, India, Thailand, and Malaysia. Specifically, in eighteen studies conducted in domestic sales contexts, twelve of them conducted their surveys among American salespeople or companies (Agnihotri et al., 2016; Guesalaga, 2016; Levin et al., 2012; Moore et al., 2013; Moore et al., 2015; Ogilvie et al., 2018; Rapp et al., 2011; Rodriguez et al., 2013; Rollins et al., 2014; Schultz et al., 2012; Trainor et al., 2014; Y. Wang et al., 2016). In addition to the research conducted in the U.S., there are two studies collecting data from India (Agnihotri et al., 2017; Itani et al., 2017), one from Thailand (Charoensukmongkol & Sasatanun, 2017), one from Malaysia (Ainin et al., 2015), and one from France (Lacoste, 2016). In Groza et al. (2012)'s research, although they collected data from 40 countries including the U.S., U.K., Germany, Canada, and other countries, 51% of the sample in their study came from the U.S. To summarize, most studies about social media use in sales conducted in domestic sales contexts tended to be limited to a number of countries, and the majority of them are based in the U.S.. A summary of research contexts about social media use in sales are presented in Table 2.3.

Table 2.3 Summary of Research Contexts about Social Media Use in Sales

Authors	Sales Contexts Domestic	Sales Contexts International	Sales Contexts Domestic & International	Samples and Data Collection Methods	Research Findings
Groza et al. (2012)	√			Data were collected from 1699 B2B salespeople from 40 countries, e.g. U.S, U.K., Germany, Australia, and Canada	Salesperson's social media use contributes to the firm's sales performance and the effect is enhanced by developmental training in the organization
Levin et al. (2012)	√			A quasi-experiment imitated sales context on an American campus and enrolled 194 business students as participants	Motivations, voluntariness, and past performance influence new sales employees' participation in social media use
Marshall et al. (2012)			√	A cross-national qualitative research was made, collecting data from two focus groups in the U.S. and two in the U.K.	Research finds that social media brings great connectivity for salespeople and customers, acts as a generational and global sales/marketing interface, brings a revolution in the buyer–seller relationship and is identified as a dominant selling tool
Rodriguez et al. (2013)	√			Data were collected from 1699 B2B salespeople in the U.S.	B2B selling organizations' social media usage has a positive relationship with their ability to create sales opportunities and manage relationships. In terms of performance, the study found that social media usage has a positive relationship with relationship sales performance, but not outcome-based sales performance
Schultz et al. (2012)	√			Data were collected from 273 B2B sales professionals in the U.S.	Age negatively affects social media usage, while social media norms positively affect it. The younger a salesperson is, the more likely he will use social media in sales. A salesperson's customers, competitors, peer salespeople, and supervisors' social media use have an influence on his adoption as well

Continued

Authors	Sales Contexts			Samples and Data Collection Methods	Research Findings
	Domestic	International	Domestic & International		
Moore et al. (2013)	✓			Data were collected from 395 salespeople in B2B and B2C markets in the U.S.	B2B managers are significantly and far more engaged with social CRM than sales representatives. The frequency and extent of social CRM usage vary based on the specific tools used and the stage of the selling process
Rapp et al. (2013)	✓			Data were collected from 28 salespeople, 144 retailers and 445 consumers in the U.S.	The effect of supplier social media usage on retailer social media usage and in turn on customer social media usage is moderated by brand reputation and service ambidexterity
Rollins et al. (2014)	✓			Researchers adopted a non-participant netnographic technique and collected 200 personal blogs from salespeople in the U.S. as data	Writing and reading blogs can be a helpful learning tool for many salespeople and companies should consider using blogging as a sales training tool
Trainor et al. (2014)	✓			Data were collected from members of top-management teams of 308 organizations in the U.S.	The research finds that a firm's social media technology use, when viewed as a resource, improves its social CRM capabilities, which positively influences customer relationship performance
Alarcón-del-Amo et al. (2015)		✓		Data were collected from 152 Spanish Exporting companies	Social media competency (SMC) has an influence on the firm's actual use of these social media applications, which in turn has an impact on the firm's performance. The intention to use social media applications mediates the relationship between the firm's SMC and its social media usage

Continued

Authors	Sales Contexts			Samples and Data Collection Methods	Research Findings
	Domestic	International	Domestic & International		
Moore et al. (2015)	✓			Data were collected from 395 sales professionals in the U.S.	A substantial proportion of B2B and B2C salespeople find utility in SM use. B2B managers are significantly and far more engaged with social CRM than sales representatives. The frequency and extent of social CRM usage vary based on the specific tools used and the stage of the selling process
Alarcón-del-Amo et al. (2016)		✓		Data were collected from 152 Spanish exporting companies	Managers' beliefs about social media capabilities for dealing with foreign customers directly influence managerial attitudes toward and intention to use social media, and also indirectly on the intention to use them through the attitude
Agnihotri et al. (2016)	✓			Data were collected from 111 sales professionals in the U.S.	Salesperson's social media use is an antecedent of enhancing salesperson behaviors to increase customer satisfaction. Their social media use is found to enhance information communication behaviors, which improve salesperson responsiveness and customer satisfaction
Guesalaga (2016)	✓			Data were collected from 220 B2B sales executives in the U.S.	Organizational competence and commitment to social media are key determinants of social media usage in sales, as well as individual commitment to it. Customer engagement with social media also predicts social media usage in sales, both directly and (mostly) through the individual and organizational factors analyzed, especially organizational competence and commitment

Continued

Authors	Sales Contexts			Samples and Data Collection Methods	Research Findings
	Domestic	International	Domestic & International		
Järvinen and Taiminen (2016)			✓	Data were collected from 4 marketing managers, 2 sales managers, and 3 experts in a large global company headquartered in Finland	The use of marketing automation (involves social media marketing) generates high quality sales leads through behavioral targeting and content personalization
Lacoste (2016)	✓			Data were collected from the top 40 French companies	The research presents a model of how key account managers (KAM) use social media, its benefits, and major issues. A key finding differentiates the use of social media by KAM versus salespeople, as KAM does not rely on social media to nurture relationships
Quinton and Wilson (2016)			✓	Data were collected from 554 dynamic interactions between professionals on selected LinkedIn wine groups and 12 interviews with wine industry experts across Australia, Asia, Europe, and the U.S.	The use of a particular professional social media platform LinkedIn helps develop business relationships and enhance business performance. Four key tensions and ties exist in the literature : relational versus transactional exchanges, emergent versus strategic social media network development, the pace of social media network formation versus the development of trust, and the notions of sharing and reciprocity versus competitive advantage
Y. Wang et al. (2016)	✓			Data were collected from 190 sellers in the U.S.	Sellers' social identity and social comparison are key factors motivating them to develop a series of co-innovation activities in an online community context (LinkedIn)
Agnihotri et al. (2017)	✓			Data were collected from 162 salespeople–customer dyads in India	Salespeople using CRM technology in conjunction with social media are more likely to exhibit higher levels of salespeople service behaviors than their counterparts with low social media technology use

Continued

Authors	Sales Contexts			Samples and Data Collection Methods	Research Findings
	Domestic	International	Domestic & International		
Bocconcelli et al. (2017)			✓	Data were collected from an Italian SME machinery company with sales in both domestic (Italy) and foreign markets	Social media is identified as an innovative resource in SMEs' sales process mainly with regard to first contact and communication activities, and a strategic resource to implement an effective business networking effort
Charoensukmongkol and Sasatanun (2017)	✓			Data were collected from 217 owners of micro-enterprises in Thailand	Entrepreneurs who used social media intensively for CRM tended to report higher satisfaction with their business performance. The positive relationship between social media use intensity for CRM and business performance satisfaction tended to be significantly higher for the entrepreneurs who exhibited lower levels of social competency in business, as well as for the companies that generated more sales from social media
Itani et al. (2017)	✓			Data were collected from 120 salesperson–supervisor dyads in India	A salesperson's goal orientation and attitude toward social media interact to positively influence social media use. A salesperson's attitude toward social media usefulness, as well as a salesperson's learning orientation, will influence how much a salesperson uses social media to assist in day-to-day job tasks
Ogilvie et al. (2018)	✓			Data were collected from 375 salespeople in the U.S.	Salespeople's social media technology use enhances their communication and adaptability behaviors
Ainin et al. (2015)	✓			Data were collected from 259 SMEs in Malaysia	Factors such as compatibility, cost-effectiveness, and interactivity influence Facebook usage among sampled SMEs. Facebook usage positively influences SMEs' financial performance and non-financial performance regarding cost reduction on marketing and customer service, improved customer relations, and improved information accessibility

Although there are many studies conducted on social media use in sales (Alarcón-del-Amo et al., 2016; Alarcón-del-Amo et al., 2015; Itani et al., 2017; Okazaki & Taylor, 2013), scholars have pointed out that there is a paucity of research about social media use in export sales (Alarcón-del-Amo et al., 2016; Alarcón-del-Amo et al., 2015; Bocconcelli et al., 2017). They argued that social media can be a "panacea" for export sales in that it helps overcome both time and spatial barriers in exporting contexts. Therefore, they called for more in-depth research on social media use in export sales (Alarcón-del-Amo et al., 2016; Alarcón-del-Amo et al., 2015; Mathews et al., 2012).

Facing the dominant U.S.-based research about social media use in sales, scholars like Okazaki & Taylor (2013) and Itani et al. (2017) have addressed the importance of more relevant research in non-U.S. contexts. Berthon et al. (2012) argued that the popularity of social media types and how social media are used in a particular country are determined by technology (such as the availability of bandwidth and its speed), culture (shared norms and values), and government (institutional rules and regulations about social media). They hold that social media usage must be adapted to different markets so that cultural factors should be taken into account. In other words, the strategies of social media use applicable in domestic sales contexts in a given country may not work in international sales contexts or in another country. Therefore, more in-depth research on social media use in sales in non-U.S. contexts is needed to have a whole picture on social media use in sales worldwide (Itani et al., 2017; Okazaki & Taylor, 2013).

Scholars who reviewed research in this area also addressed the importance of selecting salespeople from BRICS countries (Brazil, Russia, India, China, and South Africa) for research on social media use in sales (Itani et al.,2017; LaPlaca,2011). They hold that BRICS countries have exhibited the fastest-growing economic growth in the world and are "responsible for a considerable part of the goods and services consumed globally and intensely trade with one another" (LaPlaca, 2011). Studies about salespeople from any of the BRICS countries are supposed to provide valuable implications for managers interested in understanding the sales management process in non-western settings(Itani et al., 2017). In response to calls for more research in BRICS countries, this study focuses on the social media use of salespeople in China, which is one of the major BRICS countries. Moreover, China is suitable for research about social media use in export selling because it has the largest number of active social media users in the world (WeChat, 2019) and implements an export-oriented economic development policy (Yan et al., 2018). To the best of the author's knowledge, this research is among the early studies to explore the working mechanism of the possible impact of Chinese export salespeople's social media use in sales on their performance. This study views salesperson performance as the main dependent variable and will review the literature about it in the next section.

2.2 Salesperson's Performance

Salesperson's performance refers to the sales results that a salesperson achieves through the deployment of effort and skills (E. Anderson & Oliver, 1987; Román & Iacobucci, 2010). In general, it is a multi-dimensional concept (A. T. Barker, 1999; Kwak et al., 2019; Oliver & Anderson, 1994; Panagopoulos & Avlonitis, 2010) and is often measured and reflected through two dimensions which are outcome performance and behavior performance (E. Anderson & Oliver, 1987; Babakus et al., 1996; Baldauf & Cravens, 2002; Madhani, 2015). The outcome performance represents what a salesperson produces in terms of his contribution to organizational goals (e.g. sales unit, quota achievement, market share, increases in sales productivity, dollar volume, etc.)(E. Anderson & Oliver, 1987; Babakus et al., 1996; Behrman & Perreault Jr., 1982).Scholars also use terms like salesperson outcome-based performance (Rodriguez & Honeycutt Jr., 2011; Rodriguez et al., 2013), sales performance (Agnihotri et al., 2016; Banin et al., 2016), or job performance (R. E. Anderson et al., 2005) to express similar meaning. Behavior performance refers to what a salesperson does, i.e., behaviors in meeting his job responsibilities (E. Anderson & Oliver, 1987; Behrman & Perreault Jr., 1982; Piercy et al., 2012). Example activities of behavior performance include sales planning, sales reports, sales presentations, the use of technical knowledge, teamwork etc(Babakus et al., 1996; Behrman & Perreault Jr., 1982).

Later, realizing the importance of customer retention and closer customer relationships in relational sales contexts, Hunter and Perreault Jr. (2007) further decomposed the behavior dimension of a salesperson's performance into administrative performance and relationship-building performance with customers. According to Hunter and Perreault Jr. (2007), administrative performance refers to a salesperson's ability to complete his or her required non-selling related activities in a timely manner, such as submitting required reports to managers on time. Relationship-building performance with customers refers to the extent to which a salesperson performs activities to cultivate a relationship that mutually benefits the selling and buying firms. Alternative terms in sales literature are relationship performance (Rodriguez et al., 2013) and customer relationship performance (Agnihotri et al., 2012; Ogilvie et al., 2018). This study will hereafter use relationship performance for conciseness and clearness. In comparison, outcome performance and relationship performance are more customer-centric and externally focused behaviors whereas administrative performance is non-customer-centric and more internally focused (Geiger & Turley, 2006; Hunter & Perreault Jr., 2007; Zallocco et al., 2009). Therefore, they draw different levels of attention from scholars with diverse research focus and the choice of specific dimensions of salesperson performance varies across studies.

Sales literature finds a plethora of research focuses on the outcome dimension of a salesperson's performance (e.g Román & Iacobucci, 2010; Román & Rodríguez, 2015; Rapp et al., 2008; Brown & Peterson, 1993; Schultz et al., 2012; Nowlin et al., 2018 ; Challagalla & Shervani, 1996; Cravens et al., 1993; Fred Miao & Evans, 2007; Jaramillo & Grisaffe, 2009; Pettijohn et al., 2007; Sujan et al., 1994; Jones et al., 2007; Keillor et al., 2000; Miao & Evans, 2013).To name a few, Rapp, Agnihotri, and Forbes (2008) regarded the outcome-based measure of the percentage of quota as a salesperson's performance when they examined the impact of sales technology usage on a salesperson's performance. By the same token, Schultz et al. (2012) investigated the impact of B2B salespeople's social media use on their outcome performance and they operationalized it as the extent to which salespeople achieve their sales objectives. Outcome performance attracts the most attention from scholars in that the major percentage of a firm's revenue comes from the act of selling, and outcome performance is tantamount to a firm's overall success. Hence, it is often regarded as one of the most important indicators to measure a salesperson's performance (E. Anderson & Oliver, 1987; Cravens et al., 1993; MacKenzie et al., 1993; Piercy et al., 2012).

Apart from the overwhelming concern about outcome performance, other scholars use different combinations of dimensions to measure salesperson's performance according to their distinctive research objective or focus. For example, Hunter and Perreault Jr. (2007) emphasized the importance of relationship-forging tasks in a relational sales context and focused on relationship and administrative dimensions to investigate the influence of sales technology use on the salesperson's performance. In Sundaram, Schwarz, Jones, and Chin (2007)'s study, they addressed the importance of information technology in salespeople's expertise and focused on how salespeople's information technology use can improve their performance. They defined salesperson's performance in terms of IT-enabled administrative performance and IT-enabled sales performance. The former refers to the extent to which the information technology affects the quality of the salesperson's administrative tasks such as call planning and time and expense management. The latter is operationalized as the extent to which the information technology affects the quality of the salesperson's ability to produce key sales results such as exceeding the sales targets and selling high-profit margin products, etc. Though the two definitions are more specific to performance related to information technology, they still focus on the outcome and administrative dimensions of the salesperson's performance.

Given that the objective of the present study is to examine whether social media use contributes to salesperson's performance, this study focuses on outcome and relationship dimensions. Such a practice has been adopted by previous sales scholars(Rodriguez et al., 2013). For example, when examining social media usage's impact on B2B sales performance, Rodriguez et al. (2013) decomposed the sales performance into two constructs: outcome-based sales performance and relationship sales performance. Their research finds that salespeople's social media use contributes to their relationship sales performance but not outcome-based sales performance.

Based on prior researchers' findings, this study argues that factors like adaptive selling behaviors, salesperson's customer qualification skills, and CQ may have an impact on the salesperson's performance (Itani et al., 2017; Ogilvie et al., 2018; Pandey & Charoensukmongkol, 2019; Román & Iacobucci, 2010). The following part will review the literature about adaptive selling behaviors, salesperson's customer-qualification skills, and CQ in sequence.

2.3 Adaptive Selling Behaviors

2.3.1 Definition of Adaptive Selling Behaviors

Weitz et al. (1986) defined adaptive selling behaviors as "the altering of sales behaviors during a customer interaction or across customer interactions based on perceived information about the nature of the selling situation". Salespeople who use the "canned" or the standardized sales presentation across sales encounters exhibit a low level of adaptive selling, whereas those who adjust to make different sales presentations during the sales encounters show a high level of adaptive selling (Spiro & Weitz, 1990). In sales encounters, salespeople need to take a series of steps to perform adaptive selling behaviors. Weitz (1978) summarized five major steps in sales processes and proposed an ISTEA sales process model to delineate how salespeople make adjustments in sales processes. According to the model, salespeople undertake the following five activities: impression formulation (I), strategy formulation (S), transmitting messages (T), evaluating reactions (E), and making appropriate adjustments (A). An illustration of the ISTEA sales process is introduced as follows.

ISTEA sales process model starts with the impression formation activity. At this step, a salesperson develops his initial impression of the potential prospect for the first interaction according to the information derived from past experience or by observing the prospect during the interaction (Weitz, 1978). Then, according to the impression he develops about the customer, the salesperson develops a communication strategy by choosing a strategic objective and formulating specific message formats and methods to achieve it (Weitz, 1978). Next, the salesperson communicates the messages to the customer, implementing the selected communication strategy (Weitz, 1978). After this, the salesperson will evaluate the effect of the strategy implementation by observing the customer's reactions and soliciting his opinions. If the strategic objective is not achieved, the salesperson will make adjustments to change his communication strategy (Weitz, 1981). During interactions, he may need to modify his impression, change the implementation method, and alter his communication style based on the evaluation of previous interactions (Weitz, 1978). The salesperson keeps making iterative adjustments during interactions, trying to achieve his objective (Spiro & Weitz, 1990). Figure 2.1 summarizes the ISTEA sales process model in a flow chart.

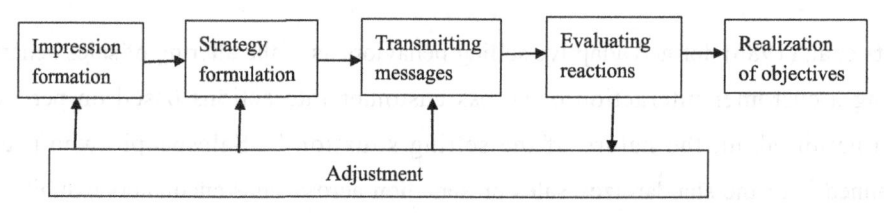

Figure 2.1 ISTEA Sales Process Model (Adapted from Weitz [1978])

However, as Spiro and Weitz (1990) pointed out, adaptive selling behavior can be undertaken in an effective and ineffective way. That is to say, adaptive selling behavior does not necessarily guarantee the effectiveness of the sales behavior, nor does its benefits outweigh its costs for sure. Literature has documented mixed research findings about the effectiveness of adaptive selling behaviors (Ahearne et al., 2005). The following part will present a detailed review about the outcomes of adaptive selling behaviors.

2.3.2 Outcomes of Adaptive Selling Behaviors

Regarding outcomes of adaptive selling behaviors, scholars have explored the contribution of adaptive selling behaviors to salespeople's performance (Chakrabarty et al., 2014; Y.-c. Chen et al., 2018; Franke & Park, 2006; Itani et al., 2017; Robinson

Jr et al., 2005; Sujan et al., 1994; Weitz et al., 1986), salespeople's job satisfaction (Chakrabarty et al., 2014; Franke & Park, 2006; Robinson Jr. et al., 2005), customer loyalty (C.-C. Chen & Jaramillo, 2014), customer satisfaction(Román & Iacobucci, 2010), rapport building (Kaski et al., 2018; Weitz, 1981), empathy(Limbu et al., 2016), trust, and so on (Guenzi et al., 2016). Among these outcomes, sales scholars like Simintiras, Ifie, Watkins, and Georgakas (2013) and Román and Iacobucci (2010) claim that one primary benefit of adaptive selling behaviors is the improved sales performance. A large body of research has explored the impact of adaptive selling behaviors on sales performance and most researchers have found direct or indirect positive relationships between them in various contexts (e.g. Weitz et al., 1986; Franke & Park, 2006; Robins et al., 2005; Chakrabarty et al., 2014; Itani et al., 2017; Román & Iacobucci, 2010). For example, Franke and Park (2006) made a meta-analysis of previous research findings related to the impact of adaptive selling behaviors on sales performance. Their meta-analysis research concluded that native English-speaking sales people's adaptive selling behaviors do make a direct contribution to the self-rated, manager-rated, and objective measures of sales performance. Despite this, when Kaynak, Kara, Chow, and Laukkanen (2016) made a cross-country comparison about the impact of salespeople's adaptive selling behaviors on their sales performance, they found a direct relationship between them in the sample of salespeople located in Macau; however, the relationship between adaptive selling behaviors and sales performance was mediated by salesperson satisfaction for the sample of salespeople in Finland. Interestingly, even in the same industry in different countries, scholars reported totally different research findings about the impact of adaptive selling behaviors on salespeople's performance (Abu ELSamen & Akroush, 2018; R. Singh & Das, 2013). For instance, in the context of the insurance industry in Jordan, Abu ELSamen and Akroush (2018)'s research found only adaptive selling behavior is not adequate for explaining salespeople's performance and the positive relationship between them must be connected by customer orientation. However, in the same industry in India, R. Singh and Das (2013)'s research found that although customer orientation plays an important middleman role in the positive effect of adaptive selling behaviors on salespeople's performance, adaptive selling behaviors alone can contribute to salespeople's performance to some extent.

In addition to research findings showing the direct and indirect impacts of adaptive selling behaviors on salespeople's performance, a small number of studies found no significant relationship between them (e.g. Ahearne et al., 2005; Pettijohn et al., 2000; Keillor et al., 2000). For example, Ahearne et al. (2005)'s research found that salespeople's adaptive selling behaviors bear no significant relationship with their job performance measured by the level of sales quota achieved. Pettijohn et al. (2000)'s research also noted that salespeople's adaptive selling behavior is only related to their own rated performance and customer-rated performance of salespeople, but it is not related to salespeople's objective performance measured by sales volume. One possible reason to explain the mixed results about the impact of adaptive selling behaviors on salespeople's performance can be sales contexts. In other words, whether and to what extent adaptive selling will contribute to salespeople's performance may be highly contingent on sales context (Keillor et al., 2000).

2.3.3 Antecedents of Adaptive Selling Behaviors

To better understand factors impacting salespeople's adaptive selling behaviors and contingent factors improving or impeding its effectiveness in various sales situations, sales scholars have identified a plethora of antecedents of adaptive selling behaviors from the perspective of characteristics of firms and characteristics of salespeople (e.g. Weitz et al., 1986; Franke & Park, 2006). Literature shows that characteristics of firms like the guidance of corporate management, sales management policies, salesperson-manager relationship quality, and behavior-based control system in terms of monitoring, directing, rewarding, and evaluation are predictors of salespeople's adaptive selling behaviors (e.g. Román & Iacobucci, 2010; Grant & Cravens, 1996; Piercy et al., 1998; Rapp et al., 2006; Rapp et al., 2008; DelVecchio, 1998; Park & Holloway, 2003). However, characteristics of salespeople such as salespeople's knowledge, goal orientation, learning orientation, selling abilities, motives, introspection, emotional intelligence (EQ), and customer-qualification skills have been identified as antecedents of salespeople's adaptive selling (e.g. Kadic-Maglajlic et al., 2016; Giacobbe et al., 2006; Porter & Inks, 2000; Román & Iacobucci, 2010; Boorom et al., 1998; Levy & Sharma, 1994; Park & Holloway, 2003; Spiro & Weitz,

1990; Sujan et al., 1994; Verbeke et al., 2004).

In recent years, as information technology has developed fast and exerted great influence on people's lives and work, its influence has penetrated the sales industry as well (Ahearne et al., 2008). Information technology has been used by salespeople in their jobs (Ahearne et al., 2008). One typical example of such technology is sales force automation tools, which can be used for sales forecasting, leads management, CRM, and sales management (Tanner Jr et al., 2005). Given this, sales scholars begin to explore the influence of information technology in the sales industry (Ahearne et al., 2008; Jones et al., 2005; Tanner Jr. et al., 2005). In personal selling, sales scholars contend that technology alone is not enough for a salesperson to reap good sales performance. Technology works by influencing a salesperson's behavior first (Ahearne et al., 2008). A stream of sales scholars focuses on the exploration of the influence of information technology on salespeople's behaviors (Ahearne et al., 2008; Robinson Jr. et al., 2005). To be specific, salespeople's use of information technology to assist in performing sales tasks has been identified as a predictive factor of their adaptive selling behaviors and efforts (Itani et al., 2017; Rapp et al., 2008). For instance, Rapp et al. (2008) reported that the usage of healthcare CRM technology tools facilitated adaptive selling behaviors of American salespeople. Recently, in view of the pervasiveness of social media, sales scholars have explored the influence of salespeople's social media use in sales on their behaviors (Itani et al., 2017; Ogilvie et al., 2018). Their studies find that salespeople's social media use in sales is beneficial to the improvement of their adaptive selling behaviors in Indian and American sales contexts. Following this stream of research, this study will retest the effect of social media use in sales on adaptive selling behaviors in Chinese export selling.

All in all, the literature shows not only characteristics of the firms and salespeople are identified as antecedents of adaptive selling behaviors, but also salespeople's and firms' integration of information technology in selling can be factors influencing salespeople's adaptive selling behaviors, which warrants up-to-date research due to the continuous advancement of information technology (Ahearne et al., 2008).

2.4 Salesperson's Customer-Qualification Skills

When salespeople interact with customers in personal selling, they need to process lots of information about customers and the selling environment (A. Sharma & Levy, 1995). To aid in information processing, salespeople need to acquire some basic skills to make this process efficient so that they can quickly identify customers' needs and buying intentions. A salesperson's customer-qualification skill is such a basic skill necessary for a salesperson to make his devotion of time and effort efficient and worthwhile. The reason supporting this argument is that customer-qualification skills help reduce the complexity of the selling proposition and communications and "free up" salespeople's mental capacity (Román & Iacobucci, 2010; Román & Rodríguez, 2015; Sujan & Bettman, 1988).

According to Román and Iacobucci (2010), a salesperson's customer-qualification skills refer to a salesperson's learned proficiency in qualifying or categorizing prospects and customers. To be specific, it is a salesperson's ability to identify and categorize different types of customers, their associated products and selling requirements. In nature, this skill is based on categorization, a cognitive ability fundamental to human beings (A. Sharma & Levy, 1995). In selling, the customer typology based on categorization can help salespeople predict customers' preferences or likely behaviors (Román & Iacobucci, 2010). The underlying assumption of this typology is that people of a certain type will behave in a manner consistent with that of other members of a similar category (Szymanski, 1988; Szymanski & Churchill, 1990).

When salespeople interact with customers, whether their categorization of a customer is correct or not depends on the level of their customer-qualification skills (Weitz et al., 1986). Further, their categorization of customers is based on the cues from incoming information during interactions with customers (Román & Iacobucci, 2010). Salespeople with a high level of customer-qualification skills are likely to make a more accurate typology of customers by categorizing sales encounters according to attributes suggesting appropriate selling strategies, whereas salespeople with a low level of customer-qualification skills are likely to classify customers according to attributes which suggest surface similarities between customers, such as their titles, genders, styles of dress, or positions in firms (Weitz et al., 1986). The accurate typology of customers helps salespeople identify and analyze customers' needs, thereby helping salespeople to have a better understanding about customers' buying motives as well as allowing them to make a better prediction about customers' buying behaviors accordingly (Román & Iacobucci, 2010; Román & Rodríguez, 2015; A. Sharma & Levy, 1995). Therefore, a salesperson with a high level of customer-qualification skills is characterized with a more accurate classification of customers and a better understanding of customer requirements (Román & Iacobucci, 2010).

Factors influencing a salesperson's customer-qualification skills include the firm's customer orientation, salesperson's intrinsic motivation, and salesperson's information technology use (Román & Iacobucci, 2010; Román & Rodríguez, 2015). For instance, Román and Rodriguez (2015)'s research drew on job demand-resource (JDR) theory to explore the influence of salespeople's information technology use on customer qualification skills. According to the JDR theory, job resources can play an intrinsic motivational potential to foster employees' growth, learning, and performance (Bakker & Demerouti, 2007). Following the theory, the authors regarded sales automation information technology as a kind of job resource available for salespeople and customer-qualification skills as salespeople's learning. The authors argued that salespeople's information technology use helps improve their customer-qualification skills because they can take full advantage of computerized memory of customer information to categorize customers and their needs. Their research findings support their argument and confirm the positive contribution of salespeople's information technology use to their customer-qualification skills (Román & Rodríguez, 2015).

In terms of the outcome of salespeople's customer-qualification skills, previous studies have explored its important role in improving customer-oriented selling, adaptive selling behaviors, and salesperson's outcome performance as well (Román & Iacobucci, 2010; Román & Rodríguez, 2015). For instance, Román and Rodríguez (2015) utilized skills-behavior-performance framework to examine the influence of salespeople's customer-qualification skills on their customer-oriented selling and outcome performance. They argued that because salespeople with stronger customer-qualification skills have a more appropriate typology of customers and better understanding of customers' needs, they can better practice customer-oriented selling by proposing appropriate solutions to meet customers' needs. In this way, they are more likely to perform customer-oriented selling and reap good outcome performance. So, customer-qualification skills are critical and necessary for salespeople to achieve effectiveness and efficiency in their personal selling (Román & Iacobucci, 2010; Román & Rodríguez, 2015).

2.5 Cultural Intelligence(CQ)

In nature, personal selling is a personal communication in which a salesperson seeks to inform buyers about products and services in an exchange situation (Pride & Ferrell, 2008). However, in export selling, as cultural differences between countries may cause misunderstanding, conflict, and disintegration, they pose great threats and barriers for a salesperson to make this personal communication proceed smoothly (Hofstede, 2001; Sozbilir & Yesil, 2016). There is a widely acknowledged complexity of managing cross-cultural communication effectively (Ang & Inkpen, 2008). Recently, cultural intelligence (CQ), a vital cross-cultural competency, has been proposed for individuals to deal with this complexity in cross-cultural communication (Charoensukmongkol, 2016a; Sozbilir & Yesil, 2016). CQ is a multi-facet concept targeted at situations involving cross-cultural interactions arising from differences in race, ethnicity, and nationality (Ang et al., 2007). Scholars have argued that it is an important skill for everyone involved in cross-cultural settings (Ang et al., 2008; D. Thomas & Inkson, 2004).

The term cultural intelligence (CQ) was first formally introduced by Earley and Ang in 2003. Based on Sternberg and Detterman (1986)'s theories about intelligence, they regarded CQ as a multidimensional conceptual construct and defined it as an individual's capability to adapt effectively to new cultural contexts (Earley & Ang, 2003). Ever since their introduction of the concept, different scholars have proposed their own definitions from different perspectives (D. Thomas & Inkson, 2004; D. C. Thomas et al., 2008). For instance, D. C. Thomas et al. (2008) drew on theories about intelligence, social cognition and cross-cultural interactions to stress CQ as a system of interacting abilities. They defined it as "a system of interacting knowledge and skills, linked by cultural metacognition, which allows people to adapt to, select, and shape the cultural aspects of their environment" (D. C.Thomas et al., 2008). They posited only three constituent components of CQ, i.e. cultural knowledge, cross-cultural skills, and cultural metacognition. In view of the wide acceptance of Earley and Ang (2003)'s definition of CQ in management research (Charoensukmongkol, 2015a, 2016a; Hansen et al., 2011; D. C. Thomas et al., 2008), this study keeps in alignment with prior researchers and adopts Earley and Ang (2003)'s ideas for hypothesis development.

According to Earley and Ang (2003), CQ is an aggregate multidimensional construct and consists of four dimensions which are cognitive CQ, metacognitive CQ, motivational CQ, and behavioral CQ. These four dimensions individually represent different capabilities and together form the overall CQ (Ang et al., 2008). Detailed meanings of the four constituent components of CQ are introduced as follows.

Cognitive CQ refers to an individual's level of cultural knowledge or knowledge of the cultural environment (Ang et al., 2008). Cultural knowledge or knowledge of the cultural environment consists of norms, practices, and conventions in different cultures like economic, legal, sociolinguistic, and interpersonal systems of different cultures, subcultures, and knowledge of basic frameworks of cultural values (Hofstede, 2001). People equipped with high levels of cognitive CQ will better understand different societies' cultures and better appreciate the systems that shape and cause specific patterns of social interaction within a culture, consequently, they will have better interactions with people from a culturally different society (Hansen et al., 2011). It is worth noting that although cognitive CQ refers to knowledge about different cultures, it is not only confined to knowledge about a specific culture but indicates knowledge of cultural universals and knowledge of cultural differences as well (Ang et al., 2007). Cognitive CQ can be acquired in direct ways like from personal experiences and in indirect ways like from educational experiences (Ang et al., 2008).

Metacognitive CQ refers to an individual's level of conscious cultural awareness during cross-cultural interactions (Ang et al., 2008). It involves control over one's cognition or thought processes (Ang et al., 2007). It promotes individuals' information processing at a deeper cognitive level and helps them develop new models, rules, and knowledge for social interaction in novel cultural environments (Earley & Ang, 2003). Relevant capabilities of metacognitive CQ include planning, monitoring, and revising one's own mental models of cultural norms for different countries or groups of people (Ang et al., 2007). Metacognitive CQ is regarded as a critical component of CQ as it involves people's deeper mental processing and active thinking about similarities and differences between cultures, doubts about previous thinking and assumptions bound on their own cultures (Ang et al., 2008). These mental activities may trigger individuals to alter or adjust their own thinking and behaviors about appropriateness in intercultural communication (Triandis, 2006). People with a high level of metacognitive CQ will consciously think about their own cultural assumptions, and different societies' cultural preferences and norms, reflect their own behavior in cross-cultural interactions, and adjust their cultural knowledge when interacting with people from different cultures so that they will achieve desired outcomes in cross-cultural interactions (Ang et al., 2008). The difference between metacognitive CQ and cognitive CQ is that the former emphasizes conscious cognitive processes in the human brain, but the latter focuses on cultural knowledge itself. Cognitive CQ can be a part of the content on which the mental processing activities are based. In this sense, cognitive CQ is also a critical component of CQ as it may serve as a basis for other components of CQ.

Motivational CQ reflects the capability to direct attention and energy toward learning and functioning in situations characterized by cultural differences (Ang et al., 2008). People with a high level of motivational CQ will be more likely and more readily in psychology to learn and engage in cross-cultural interaction when confronted with conflicts in different cultural situations (Chen et al., 2012). According to the expectancy-value theory of motivation (Eccles & Wigfield, 2002), when individuals are performing a task, the expectation of successfully accomplishing the task and the value associated with accomplishing it will channel the direction and magnitude of energy to the completion of the task. Facing novel situations in different societies, to successfully adapt to new cultures, people need to direct their attention and energy to solve various problems caused by cultural differences (Earley & Ang, 2003). It is another critical component of CQ as it serves as a source of drive or motivation to know about other cultures. As an intrinsic interest, it triggers people's attention and energy to flow toward functioning in novel cultural settings (Ang et al., 2008).

Behavioral CQ refers to the capability to exhibit appropriate verbal and nonverbal actions when interacting with people from different cultures (Ang et al., 2008). When individuals with behavioral CQ are interacting directly in a face-to-face way with people in cross-cultural settings, they usually behave correspondingly by observing their count-partners' verbal and nonverbal behaviors (Ang & Van Dyne, 2008). Their behavioral CQ will help them exhibit verbal and nonverbal actions and transform their perception and motivations into immediate actions (Ang et al., 2007). Together with the other three components of CQ (cognitive CQ about cultural knowledge, metacognitive CQ about mental processing, and motivational CQ about intrinsic interest and motivations), behavioral CQ is the last but critical dimension to generate individuals' active engagement or involvement in cross-cultural adaptation. It is the power that transforms the willingness, motivation, and intrinsic interest into salient actions or behaviors (Hansen et al., 2011).

The appropriateness of an individual's behavior in cross-cultural interactions bears a close relationship with all four components of CQ (Ang et al., 2008). Therefore, although Earley and Ang (2003)'s theories hold that the above four components of CQ are qualitatively different dimensions of the overall capability to function and manage effectively in culturally diverse settings, it is implied that the overall CQ construct may be best conceptualized as an aggregate multidimensional construct (Ang et al., 2008).

As an intercultural competence, CQ has been mostly studied in research relevant to intercultural communication settings (Ang et al., 2008; Earley & Ang, 2003). Typically, previous CQ studies mainly choose international students, expatriates, global managers, and employees in multinational enterprises (MNEs) as their research objects, because these people's life and work involve a lot of intercultural communication activities in host countries (Adair et al., 2013; Ang & Van Dyne, 2015; Moon, 2010). For international students, CQ has been found to have a positive relationship with their task performance (Ang et al., 2007), adaptive performance (Oolders et al., 2008), cross-cultural adjustment (Lin et al., 2012), general and interaction adjustment (Chen et al., 2014), intention to work abroad (Remhof et al., 2013), intercultural cooperation (Mor et al., 2013), intercultural negotiations and negotiation outcomes (Groves et al., 2015), mental health (Ahmadi & Hoseini, 2017), individual creativity (Hu et al., 2017), language learning strategy (Rachmawaty et al., 2018) and EQ (Rahmatsyah Putranto et al., 2018). For expatriates, CQ has also been found to show a positive impact on their expatriate performance (Lee & Sukoco, 2010), job performance and effectiveness (Lee et al., 2013), general, interaction, and work adjustment (Huff et al., 2014; Malek & Budhwar, 2013). For global managers and employees in MNEs, extant studies have documented that CQ helps reduce anxiety (Bücker et al., 2014; Suthatorn & Charoensukmongkol, 2018), enhance their communication effectiveness and job satisfaction (Bücker et al., 2014), promote cross-border leadership (Rockstuhl et al., 2011), enhance cultural judgment, decision-making, and task performance (Ang et al., 2007), improve intercultural creative collaboration (Chua et al., 2012), enhance job performance and cross-cultural job satisfaction (Barakat et al., 2015; Sozbilir & Yesil, 2016), facilitate life satisfaction and career engagement (Le et al., 2018), increase creativity (Castañeda et al., 2018; Yunlu et al., 2017), develop entrepreneurship (Baltaci, 2017), and improve intercultural negotiation effectiveness (Imai & Gelfand, 2010).

In a word, academia has identified CQ as an important ability necessary in intercultural interaction settings and proved its positive impact in international business success (Crowne, 2008). However, despite that CQ is powerful in explaining intercultural communication effectiveness (Ang et al., 2007), limited research has touched upon the impact of salespeople's CQ on their intercultural selling activities or performance (Charoensukmongkol, 2019b; Chen & Jaramillo, 2014; Pandey & Charoensukmongkol, 2019).Three exceptions are Pandey and Charoensukmongkol (2019)'s, Charoensukmongkol (2019b)'s, and Chen et al. (2012)'s research. Pandey and Charoensukmongkol (2019)'s and Charoensukmongkol (2019b)'s research explicitly targets on export selling and investigates the impact of CQ on Thai salespeople's adaptive selling behaviors at international trade shows.

Chen et al. (2012)'s research focuses on an intercultural selling in America. The authors investigated the impact of American realtors' behavioral CQ on their sales performances when they sell real estate to buyers coming from diverse cultural origins. Their research found that motivational CQ helps increase American realtors' sales performance in intercultural selling. Despite its limitation in considering only one dimension of CQ, their research finding anticipates a positive role of salespeople's CQ in export selling. Given the prior evidence about the contribution of CQ in cross-cultural situations, especially in intercultural sales, this study argues that CQ might play an important role in export selling via social media.

2.6 Theories

This part will introduce two theories supporting the hypothesis development of this study which are adaptive selling theory and categorization theory. Adaptive selling theory will be introduced first as it offers theoretical support for the main conceptual framework of this research. This theory is used to explain the impact of social media use in sales, customer-qualification skills, and CQ on adaptive selling behaviors and salesperson's performance. Then, categorization theory is introduced to explain the mediating role of customer-qualification skills in the effect of social media use and CQ on adaptive selling behaviors and salesperson's performance.

2.6.1 Adaptive Selling Theory

Adaptive selling theory, also called adaptation theory, is a theoretical framework proposed by Weitz et al. (1986) in their seminal research about adaptive selling framework (Arli et al., 2018; Giacobbe et al., 2006). The theory centers on a specific ability of a salesperson, i.e. adaptive selling behavior (Weitz et al., 1986). The underlying reason why adaptive selling behavior has attracted great attention lies in the consensus between both academia and practitioners that there is no single best way to sell in view of the great complexity and uncertainty of sales encounters (Weitz et al., 1986). Salespeople should be adaptive enough in selling processes and adopt a contingency sales strategy based on their understanding about the characteristics of customers and sales situations (Román & Iacobucci, 2010; Viio & Grönroos, 2016; Weitz, 1978, 1981).

According to Weitz et al. (1986), the main arguments of the theory consist of three parts. The first part involves the positive outcome of adaptive selling behavior on salespeople's performance improvement and the moderating role of environmental conditions and salespeople's capabilities in the effect of adaptive selling behavior on salespeople's performance. Weitz et al. (1986) argued that only when the selling environment and salespeople's capabilities result in benefits outweighing the costs of practicing adaptive selling behavior, adaptive selling behavior will lead to improved sales performance. The second part involves the role of salespeople's characteristics as antecedents of adaptive selling behavior. The third part is concerned with the role of sales management variables as the antecedents of salesperson's characteristics. Scholars regard salespeople's characteristics as first-order contingencies and sales situations as second-order contingencies (Giacobbe et al., 2006; Spiro & Weitz, 1990; Weitz, 1981; Weitz et al., 1986). Both first-order and second-order contingencies influence the effectiveness of adaptive selling behavior (Giacobbe et al., 2006).

Specifically, this theory holds that a salesperson's characteristics comprise two major factors: a salesperson's motivation to practice adaptive selling behavior and his capabilities. A salesperson's motivation to practice adaptive selling behavior includes intrinsic reward orientation and strategy attribution (Weitz et al., 1986). For sales management, factors like non-contingent rewards, cognitive feedback, self-management and organizational culture facilitate the development of intrinsic reward orientation; and factors like environmental cues, cognitive feedback provided by managers and self-management are related to the salesperson's tendency to make strategy attributions (Weitz et al., 1986). Meanwhile, salesperson's capabilities consist of his abilities and skills (Weitz et al., 1986). Factors like training and selection can help improve a salesperson's abilities and skills (Weitz et al., 1986). A salesperson's capabilities can motivate the practice of adaptive selling behavior. Moreover, the higher level of capabilities a salespeople has, the more improvement of sales performance his adaptive selling behaviors will contribute to (Weitz et al., 1986).

The great contribution the adaptive selling framework has made to personal selling lies in its emphasis on the effect of salespeople's adaptive selling behavior on sales performance. Such an emphasis is significant because adaptive selling behavior is a factor that an individual salesperson can control and improve by effort (Sujan et al., 1994). Another significance of the adaptive selling framework is that it provides a comprehensive framework by identifying the characteristics of salespeople as the antecedents of adaptive selling behavior and salespeople's performance as the consequence of adaptive selling behavior (Arli et al., 2018). The analysis of sales management variables also offers valuable guidance and inspiration for both academia and practitioners in sales and marketing fields to better understand how sales management can contribute to the improvement of an individual salesperson's sales performance from the perspective of sales management. Ever since Weitz et al. (1986)'s introduction of the adaptive selling framework, adaptation theory gained momentum in its development (Giacobbe et al., 2006). Up to now, it has become one of the most influential and prominent theories in the sales and marketing fields and has been extensively investigated (Franke & Park, 2006; Kaptein et al., 2018; Román & Iacobucci, 2010).

As has been discussed in the literature review about adaptive selling, numerous sales and marketing scholars have provided empirical evidence supporting the main arguments of the adaptive selling framework, and further enriched the scope of antecedents or determinants of adaptive selling behavior by identifying more factors about characteristics of salespeople and sales organizations (Chakrabarty et al., 2004; Franke & Park, 2006; Giacobbe et al., 2006; Levy & Sharma, 1994; Park & Holloway, 2003; Pettijohn et al., 2000; Simintiras et al., 2013). For instance, Giacobbe et al. (2006) followed the adaptive selling framework to view salespeople's characteristics as first-order contingencies and operationalized salespeople's characteristics as their empathic ability toward the buyer, cue perception ability, presentation modifying skills and knowledge (operationalized as selling experience). Meanwhile, they regard selling situations as second-order contingencies and identified two selling contexts as selling situations which are "adaptive" contexts and "nonadaptive" contexts. They define the "adaptive" contexts as more complex and high-demanding selling contexts, e.g. when the offering of goods is complex or customers' needs change considerably. The "nonadaptive" contexts are in the opposite condition to "adaptive" contexts. They investigated the role of these contingencies on the effect of adaptive selling behavior on sales performance. Their empirical research findings supported the positive role of adaptive selling behavior on sales performance in both "adaptive" and "nonadaptive" selling contexts. Their research also identified the studied salesperson characteristics as determinants of the salesperson's intention to practice adaptive selling behaviors. Their research strengthened the power of the framework and offered more inspiration for further research.

This study uses adaptive selling framework as its theoretical support for hypothesis development. Drawing on the main arguments of the framework, this study would like to regard social media use, salesperson's customer-qualification skills, and CQ as characteristics of an export salesperson to explore whether these factors affect an export salesperson's adaptive selling behaviors, and in turn sales performance in the export selling context. According to Weitz et al. (1986), abilities like knowledge and skills like information acquisition skills are components of the capabilities of a salesperson. The authors argued that a salesperson needs an elaborate knowledge structure of sales situations, sales behaviors, and contingencies to practice adaptive selling effectively. To use this knowledge in selling, he needs to be skillful in collecting information about customers, their beliefs, values, situations, and contingencies (Weitz et al., 1986). This study holds that an export salesperson's social media use in sales reflects his capability in terms of information acquisition skills because social media provides a great channel accessible for exporting salespeople to collect information about their foreign customers and selling environments (Lacoste, 2016). Given this rationale, this study regards an export salesperson's social media use in sales as a component of his capabilities to practice adaptive selling behavior.

Further, because a salesperson's customer-qualification skills involve the collection of enough information about customers and represent his categorization level of customers and refined knowledge about the correct typology of customers (Román & Iacobucci, 2010), a salesperson's customer-qualification skills meet the requirement of the basic knowledge structure necessary to practice adaptive selling behaviors. Thus, this study regards customer qualification skills as a component salesperson's capability to practice adaptive selling behaviors in export selling as well.

In addition, the cross-cultural selling situation in export selling requires salespeople equipped with cultural knowledge about the importing countries and importers' customs, beliefs, and values to meet the requirement of a salesperson's basic knowledge structure about sales situations and contingencies to practice adaptive selling behaviors (Hansen et al., 2011). This study argues that CQ meets this requirement because a salesperson's CQ level mirrors the knowledge dimension of a salesperson's capabilities to practice adaptive selling behaviors. Thus, this study regards CQ as an export salesperson's another component of capability to practice adaptive selling behaviors in export selling.

Based on the above analysis, this study regards social media use, customer-qualification skills, and CQ as the important components of an export salesperson's capabilities and follows the adaptation theory to propose that these three factors are antecedents of adaptive selling behavior, which will contribute to sales performance. A simplified chart of adaptive selling framework used in this study is presented as follows in Figure 2.2.

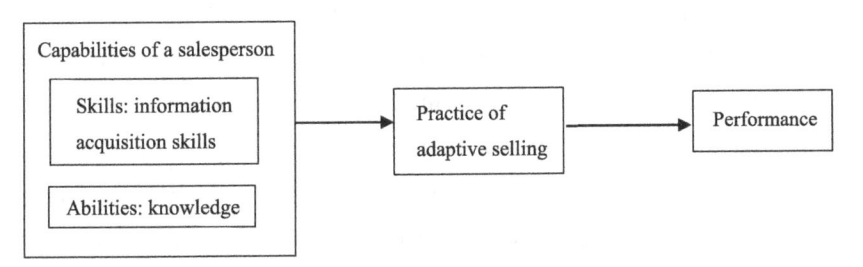

Figure 2.2 The Simplified Chart of Adaptive Selling Framework (Adapted from Weitz, Sujan [1986])

2.6.2 Categorization Theory

Categorization theory can be dated back to Aristotle's classical philosophy about categories, which holds that all category members have all of the defining features of the category and are equally good category exemplars (Mann, 2000). For example, a geometric object can be categorized as a square rather than a rectangle only when it has four equal sides joined at right angles. In other words, the membership of a category depends on possessing all the necessary and sufficient features of the category(Cantor & Mischel, 1979). This traditional all-or-none criterion for category membership fits well in the abstract world of logic and formal systems like the cited classification of rectangle and square (Cantor & Mischel, 1979). However, Wittgenstein, Anscombe, and Wittgenstein (1953) noticed that the classical view of categorization does not apply to common and everyday categories which do not share all the defined critical features for category membership. Wittgenstein et al. (1953) argued that category members show a pattern of overlapping similarities and the membership of a category represents a family resemblance structure. This idea was championed by many other linguists, psychologists, and philosophers like Labov (1973), Hedges (1972), Rosch, Mervis, Gray, Johnson, and Boyes-Braem (1976), etc. For example, the furniture category includes chairs, tables, beds, cabinets, etc. These members of the furniture category share some overlapping similarities with each other but do not all share all of the necessary and sufficient features of the furniture category. Rosch and Mervis (1975) argued that there is a prototype or stereotype which serves as the best example of a concept for every category and other less prototypical category members form a continuum away from the central prototypical exemplar. Rosch et al. (1976) and Smith, Shoben, and Rips (1974) argued that people reliably judge members of a category as being better or worse exemplars of a category. Such an idea has been widely accepted and further applied in various fields (Cantor & Mischel, 1979; D. Lee & Ganesh, 1999; Oakes et al., 1994; Offermann & Coats, 2018). When it comes to the classification of people in the social science domain, scholars argue that the categorization of people is based on a great variety of social, behavioral, and cultural categories, as well as abstract constructs like extrovert personality (Bruner et al., 1956; Cantor & Mischel, 1979; C. Cohen, 1977). For example, C. Cohen (1977) has described the prototypes of "librarian" and "waitress" based on the commonly held stereotypes of these two typical types of occupations.

Despite the continuing controversy about the categorization process, scholars reach a consensus that categorization is functional rather than structural or representational in that it helps people enhance information processing efficiency and cognitive stability by grouping objects or events together according to their similarities in important respects (Bruner et al., 1956; J. Cohen & Basu, 1987). Categorization plays an important role in people's perceptual process (Cantor & Mischel, 1979). It helps people simplify and reduce cognitive burden in a potentially complex cognitive situation with a variety of stimuli (Bruner, 1957). It guides people to selectively focus on certain aspects of particular stimuli and to group these stimuli under a unifying category label (Bruner, 1957). Based on categorization, people can predict the specific features of any category member according to the general expectations about the category (Bruner, 1957). In the social domain, the categorization of people allows perceivers to structure and link their general store of knowledge about people, which provides corresponding expectations about typical behavior patterns and a set of likely variations among different types of people and their characteristic behaviors (Cantor & Mischel, 1979). Given this, not only linguists, philosophers, and psychologists show great interest in categorization theory but also management scholars pay great attention to it and actively apply it to the management fields (Cantor & Mischel, 1979; Hedges, 1972; Labov, 1973; Loken et al., 2008; A. Sharma & Levy, 1995; Wittgenstein et al., 1953).

In management fields, categorization theory has been used to explore leadership perception (Lord et al., 1984; Lord et al., 1982; H. Nguyen et al., 2018), consumer psychology about product categories, product user categories, brand categories, cultural categories, etc.(Aaker & Lee, 2001; Alba & Hutchinson, 1987; Loken et al., 2008; Pechmann & Knight, 2002; Viswanathan & Childers, 1999). For instance, Lord et al. (1984) drew on categorization theory to build a leadership categorization theory. The leadership categorization theory identified three hierarchical structures of leadership categories (superordinate, basic, and subordinate) and explained leadership perceptions in terms of categorization and how to use properties of categories to improve other information-processing tasks. To date, the leadership categorization theory has evolved into implicit leadership theories, which postulates that people's implicit conceptualizations of leaders represent the cognitive structures specifying the expected leader traits and attributes (Offermann & Coats, 2018).

Scholars in personal selling fields apply categorization theory to investigate the effect of salespeople's categorization on their selling abilities, selling behaviors, and performance (Román & Iacobucci, 2010; A. Sharma & Levy, 1995; A. Sharma et al., 2000; Szymanski, 1988; Szymanski & Churchill Jr., 1990; Weitz, 1978; Weitz et al., 1986).For example, A. Sharma and Levy (1995) investigated retail salespeople's customer category information and identified three categorization styles retail salespeople use to classify customers which are need-based categorizers, decision styles categorizers, and training-based categorizers. Their research also found that retail salespeople use customer category information to aid in selling, positioning and promotion activities. A. Sharma et al. (2000) investigated the relationship between retail salespeople's categorization and their performance. Their research confirmed that the surveyed salespeople with higher sales performance tend to have richer category descriptions about customers, more distinctive customer category structures, more emphasis on customers' needs rather than customers' physical characteristics, and more complete and complex procedural knowledge about selling steps and sales strategies.

Szymanski (1988) pointed out that salespeople's ability to identify customers' product and selling-related needs is an antecedent of their correct classification of sales leads into sales categories at a set of selling processes like prospecting, sales presentation, and closing stages. They also found that the correct classification of sales leads is a determinant of sales performance. This finding is in line with Sujan, Weitz, and Sujan (1988)'s arguments that salespeople who can accurately classify customers and adjust their selling strategies to be more congruent with customers' types tend to reap higher performance.

In view of the great impact of salespeople's categorization on their selling behaviors and performance, Román and Iacobucci (2010) drew on categorization theory to propose a customer typology, which they argue can help salespeople identify customers' needs and predict customers' likely behavior according to their categorization of customers. They defined a new concept called the salesperson's customer qualification skills as "the salesperson's learned proficiency to qualify or categorize prospects and customers". Their research identified the important role of customer-qualification skills as an antecedent of the salesperson's adaptive selling behavior. Later, Román and Rodríguez (2015) confirmed the important mediating role of salespeople's customer-qualification skills in the effect of salespeople's technology use on outcome performance.

Given the widely acknowledged role of salesperson's categorization in their behaviors and performance, this study uses categorization theory as its theoretical support to explore the mediating role of salespersons' customer-qualification skills in the effect of social media use and CQ on adaptive selling behaviors and sales performance.

2.6.3 Social Customer Relationship Management Framework

This study also seeks to get theoretical support from the social customer relationship management (social CRM) strategic framework. Social CRM is a philosophy and a business strategy deeply rooted in relational marketing (Choudhury & Harrigan, 2014). It is defined as "the integration of customer-facing activities including processes, systems, and technologies with emergent social media applications to engage customers in collaborative conversations and enhance customer relationships" (Trainor, 2012). To create value from managed customer relationships, firms must engage in a four-step IDIC process(Identification, Differentiation, Interaction, and Customization) (Peppers & Rogers, 2016). In the first identification step, customer information like demographic characteristics, habits, preferences and purchase history, is collected to create a customer database ready for use in the later processes of CRM. Next, in the differentiation process, customers are categorized into different groups based on similar customer needs and values to the firm. Then, interactions are made with customers for further learning about details of customer needs and behaviors. This process is implemented to ensure customer expectations are understood correctly and efficiently in combination with the information in the customer database. Lastly, in the customization process, the firm adapts some aspects of behaviors to customize a product or service to meet customers' expectations according to specific needs and preferences identified in the early stages of CRM. A description of the IDIC process is illustrated in Figure 2.3.

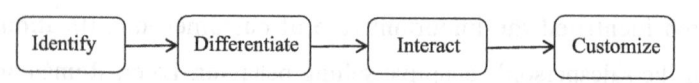

Identify → Differentiate → Interact → Customize

Figure 2.3　IDIC process of Managing Customer Relationship

According to the social CRM framework, the application of social media in customer-facing activities can lead to optimal customer relationship performance through identification, differentiation, interaction, and customization. Peppers and Rogers (2016) argued that the four implementation tasks of IDIC methodology can not only help companies create and manage customer experience and relationships, but also apply to salespeople as well. Following these scholars' studies, this study regards export salespeople's selling activities as customer-facing activities and applys this theoretical framework to explain the effect of salespeople's social media use on customer-qualification skills and adaptive selling behaviors, which in turn lead to good relationship performance.

This study argues that the four implementation tasks of the IDIC process match well with customer-qualification skills and adaptive selling behaviors. In particular, the first two processes of IDIC which are identification and differentiation represent exactly salespeople's customer-qualification processes because customer-qualification skills refer to salespeople's competency to identify and qualify customers based on customers' needs and values. The remaining two processes of IDIC which are interaction and customization mirror the practicing process of salespeople's adaptive selling behaviors in that the concept of adaptive selling behaviors itself involves iterative interactions with customers and adjustments to sales behaviors to meet distinctive customer needs.

According to social CRM, the integration of social media in export sales activities will engage foreign customers in collaborative communications with salespeople and enhance customer relationships. For instance, by integrating social media in sales processes, in the identification process, export salespeople can leverage an expansive machinery memory of customers' profiles available on social media platforms to collect a huge amount of information about customers to identify qualified customers. On the one hand, salespeople can track the records of consumers' posts in the past, like the messages that the customers wrote, the pictures that customers posted about the activities they did, the place they travelled to, their lifestyle, etc. Hence, they can have a general understanding about the characteristics and preferences of customers through the analysis of the content that consumers post on social media platforms. On the other hand, they can follow customers on social media platforms to update their beliefs and state of knowledge about customers to predict customer's behaviors. In this way, social media can act as powerful "big data" that allows salespeople to do content analysis to understand the characteristics and preferences of consumers. Based on this understanding of customers' characteristics and preferences, salespeople make a (preliminary) judgment about the customers' value, fulfilling the initial identification process.

In the differentiation process, salespeople utilize the information collected on social media to categorize foreign customers according to the preliminarily identified customer needs. In the identification and differentiation process, the integration of social media into CRM can improve the efficiency and effectiveness of customer qualification, facilitating an improvement of customer-qualification skills. For example, some social media platforms like WeChat and Facebook have a grouping function, which allows salespeople to manage and classify foreign customers in different groups. Salespeople who fully leverage the grouping function of social media develop their customer-qualification skills accordingly. Taking Facebook as an example, a salesperson can join a particular existing group which may have thousands of group members. He or she can post product information in this group and even create a poll to launch interactive communication to collect customers' opinions about products, needs, preferences, purchasing habits, etc. The salesperson develops a preliminary understanding about customers' needs and expectations from customers' responses, which help salespeople classify and qualify customers. Further, the salesperson can use the grouping function on Facebook to invite customers with similar needs to establish a new group for himself or herself. In this way, the salesperson becomes the owner of this classified customer group and has the right to manage this group. In the process of using social media functions to engage customers in interactive communication, salespeople practice identifying and differentiating customers' needs and preferences, leading to an improvement of customer-qualification skills. To summarize, on the one hand, in the first two IDIC processes, as social media can act as "big data" by providing a large amount of information for salespeople to make content analysis about customers, salespeople who fully utilize the characteristics of social media have more chances of practicing categorizing and qualifying customers. This matches well with categorization theory which holds that people categorize information to improve their cognitive efficiency and effectiveness when encountering a flux of information. That's why customer-qualification skills play an important role in export selling via social media. On the other hand, technological support like grouping functions of social media can even assist in managing customers by groups in a convenient and efficient way, which highlights the importance of integrating information technology (social media) in helping customer relationship management.

Next, in the interaction process, salespeople can fully utilize the interactive communication function of social media to engage foreign customers to express their needs and expectations. Collaborative communication on social media can help salespeople gain a clear understanding of customer needs and expectations, paving the way for salespeople to make corresponding adjustments to their behaviors. Lastly, salespeople practice adaptive selling behaviors to prescribe a customized solution based on perceptions of customer's needs and expectations, which mirrors the customization process in IDIC. Customized offers and mutual communication increase customers' trust and satisfaction, leading to optimal customer relationship performance.

Given the above rationale, this study deploys social CRM framework to underpin the main argument of the present study which proposes that social media use in sales can facilitate an improvement in customer-qualification skills and adaptive selling behaviors, which can in turn lead to good customer relationship performance. A plethora of studies have explored the contribution of social media use to the establishment of good customer relationships under the social CRM framework (Choudhury & Harrigan, 2014;

Harrigan et al., 2015; Peppers & Rogers, 2016; Trainor, 2012; Trainor et al., 2014). Marketing scholars in the fields of CRM and IT concluded that social media use is not sufficient to yield good customer relationships; instead, it must work by some mediating factors (Chang et al., 2010; Charoensukmongkol & Sasatanun, 2017; Chen et al., 2015; Choudhury & Harrigan, 2014; Harrigan et al., 2015; Sasatanun & Charoensukmongkol, 2016; Trainor, 2012; Trainor et al., 2014). For instance, Choudhury and Harrigan (2014)'s research confirmed that there was no direct significant relationship between social CRM technology (social media) use and customer relationship performance whereas there was a significant pathway between them linked by relational information process. In addition, Trainor et al. (2014)'s research drew on resources-based views and capabilities-based perspectives to regard social media use as resources to a firm and argued that social media use must be transformed into capabilities first so as to provide relationship performance gains. Their research found that a firm's social CRM capabilities in terms of information generation and information dissemination play an important role in the contribution of a firm's social media use on its customer relationship performance.

It is worth noting that although scholars often regard companies as the main actors of social CRM, scholars like Peppers and Rogers (2016) have pointed out that it is also applicable to sales force as the use of social media blurred the boundaries between marketing and sales activities and glued them in a closer relationship. Empirical evidence has been found in the literature supporting that the social CRM framework is applicable to individual salespersons (Chen et al., 2015; Sasatanun & Charoensukmongkol, 2016). For example, Sasatanun and Charoensukmongkol (2016) identified the antecedents and outcomes of social media use in customer relationship management by studying Thai microenterprises and the size of these firms varied from one to five employees. In particular, Chen et al. (2015)'s research found that individual employees who use CRM systems enable their adaptive behaviors to provide personalized service to individual customers, which in turn improves customer service performance. Thus, given the importance of integration of social media in CRM and the necessity of the underlying IDIC implementation activities to yield good customer relationships, this study uses social CRM as a theoretical framework to support the effect of social media use in sales on customer-qualification skills and adaptive selling behaviors, which can result in an enhancement in customer relationship performance.

2.7 Hypotheses Development

2.7.1 Social Media Use in Sales and Salesperson's Customer-Qualification Skills

This study proposes that an export salesperson's social media use in sales is positively related to his customer-qualification skills. The study argues for a positive link between social media use in sales and salesperson's customer-qualification skills for the following two reasons. Firstly, a salesperson needs enough information about customers and selling situations as a basis to qualify and categorize customers (Weitz et al., 1986). However, due to the great time and spatial barriers between countries, export salespeople have difficulty collecting enough information about customers and selling situations. Scholars have stressed that social media use can help overcome these barriers in export selling by offering a channel for export salespeople to get access to prospects and their relevant profiles (Alarcón-del-Amo et al., 2016; Okazaki & Taylor, 2013). In other words, export salespeople can use social media as information acquisition tools to collect information about customers and foreign countries to qualify and categorize customers. Secondly, social media is an ideal platform for salespeople to listen to customers and interact with them, facilitating the identification of customers' needs and expectations (Lacoste, 2016). Thus, this study argues that an export salesperson who has a high level of social media use in his selling processes is more likely to have the right typology of foreign customers because he can approach more customers, collect more relevant information, and better identify customer needs and expectations through social media. The huge amount of information about foreign customers and countries available on social media meets the prerequisite of an information base for customer categorization and aids in qualifying customers. Although, to date, no research has linked social media use with customer-qualification skills, the proposed relationship between them aligns with Román and Rodríguez (2015)'s research findings about the positive influence of salesperson's information technology use on the salesperson's customer-qualification skills. Given that social media has been identified as a form of information technology use which helps salespeople perform service behaviors leading to value creation (Agnihotri et al., 2012), this study holds the positive impact of the salesperson's information technology use on the salesperson's customer-qualification skills is applicable to the salesperson's social media use in sales as well. The formal hypothesis is stated as follows:

Hypothesis 1: An export salesperson's social media use in sales is positively associated with his customer-qualification skills.

2.7.2 Salesperson's Customer-Qualification Skills and Adaptive Selling Behaviors

This study proposes that a salesperson's customer-qualification skills are positively associated with his adaptive selling behaviors. Hansen et al. (2011) argued that a salesperson's knowledge structure is a factor determining the quality of his adaptive selling behaviors because adaptation requires elaborate knowledge structures of selling situations (Leong et al., 1989; A. Sharma et al., 2000; Sujan, et al., 1988). The definition of adaptive selling behaviors also suggests that a salesperson's perception about selling situations is a prerequisite for his altering presentations in sales encounters (Weitz et al., 1986). Salespeople with high customer-qualification skills meet this pre-requirement as they have richer and well-developed category knowledge about customer types. They can leverage the well-classified customer types to better organize, interpret, and evaluate sales situations, to select personalized sales strategies for well-defined customer types, and to make corresponding adjustments to meet different types of customers' needs during sales presentations (Leong et al., 1989). According to A. Sharma and Levy (1995), salespeople with a well-developed category structure practice adaptive selling behavior to a higher degree than those who do not. Román and Iacobucci (2010)'s empirical research also confirmed that salespeople's customer-qualification skills bear a positive association with their adaptive selling behaviors. Therefore, this study posits that:

Hypothesis 2: An export salesperson's customer-qualification skills are positively associated with his adaptive selling behaviors.

2.7.3 Social Media Use in Sales and Adaptive Selling Behaviors

This study proposes that an export salesperson's social media use in sales and adaptive selling behaviors is positively associated. This study argues that the level of a salesperson's integration of social media use into his sales job can reflect his information acquisition skills, an antecedent of adaptive selling behaviors. As Ogilvie et al. (2018) have pointed out, social media characterized with convenient accessibility and wide networks offers a valuable channel for export salespeople to identify a large body of prospects during the preapproach period and get to know a prospect or customer about his preferences, buying habits, and beliefs before approaching or during interactions. It is imperative for salespeople to collect enough information about sales situations, markets, and customers before approaching and during interactions to practice adaptive behavior (Weitz et al., 1986). The reachable profile of customers via social media allows salespeople to develop a deeper perception of consumers' behaviors, helpful in developing unique sales presentations for specific customers. According to Hunter and Perreault Jr. (2007), the more information salespeople have about their customers, the more likely they will adjust their presentations and practice adaptive selling.

With the development of information technology, social media can support instant message transmission in various forms such as texts, documents, voice mails, videos, pictures, etc.(Farrell & Hutasingh, 2018). Additionally, the present internet technology also equips social media with both synchronous (use at the same time) and asynchronous media characteristics (use at different time)(Moore et al., 2015) These characteristics and functions of social media make export salespeople's alteration of their selling behavior possible and convenient by offering more alternative ways to present their products and/or services during interactions with customers(Okazaki & Taylor, 2013). Recent studies have provided supportive evidence proving that salespeople's social media use improves their adaptive selling behaviors in domestic sales contexts in America and India (Itani et al., 2017; Ogilvie et al., 2018). Based on these rationales and findings in recent sales literature mentioned here, this study argues that an export salesperson's social media use in sales is conducive to his adaptive selling behaviors. Therefore, salesperson this study posits that:

Hypothesis 3: There is a positive association between an export salesperson's social media use in sales and his adaptive selling behaviors.

2.7.4 Adaptive Selling Behaviors and Salesperson's Performance

This study proposes that an export salesperson's adaptive selling behavior is positively associated with his sales performance. Ever since the introduction of Weitz's framework about adaptive selling behavior, numerous researchers have examined the positive relationship between adaptive selling behavior and salesperson's performance (e.g. Weitz et al., 1986; Sujan et al., 1994; Franke & Park, 2006; Robins Jr. et al., 2005; Chakrabarty et al., 2014 ; Giacobbe et al., 2006; Itani et al., 2017; Chen et al., 2018). The underlying reason supporting this positive relationship is that when a salesperson adopts adaptive selling behavior, he is sensitive to identifying the customer's expectations and needs by closely observing the customer's response during the communication process (Weitz et al., 1986). On the one hand, he would adjust his communication strategy to make his presentation manner friendlier and more acceptable to customers; on the other hand, he can make customized offerings about products or services to meet customers' needs and expectations (Román & Iacobucci, 2010). In this way, the salesperson's adaptive selling behavior makes customers satisfied with his offering, increasing the chance of closing a deal (Román & Iacobucci, 2010). Some scholars even argued that thanks to the long-term focus and important role of customer satisfaction in building quality relationships in B2B marketing, an adaptive selling approach enhances a salesperson's ability to build quality relationships with customers, which is conducive to increasing his sales performance as well (Itani et al., 2017; Jaramillo et al., 2007).

In export selling, great barriers in terms of both geographical distance and cultural differences require salespeople to commit more efforts to figure out and respond to foreign customer's needs and expectations as people from different cultures often have distinctive needs and preferences (Chen et al., 2012). Such requirements highlight the necessity of adaptive selling behavior in export selling. Only when an export salesperson uses the adaptive selling strategy can they satisfy foreign buyers' distinctive demands and needs and reap more orders from foreign buyers. In addition to the adaption theory's support, empirical evidence supporting a positive relationship between adaptive selling behavior and salesperson performance has also been documented in previous studies (e.g. Leong et al., 1989; Porter et al., 2003; Predmore & Bonnice, 1994; Fang et al., 2004; Franke & Park, 2006; Rapp et al., 2008; Jaramillo & Grisaffe, 2009; Kaynak et al., 2016; Ogilvie et al., 2018). To name a few, Román and Iacobucci (2010) observed the positive impact of financial services salespeople's adaptive selling behavior on their customers' satisfaction and salespeople's outcome performance in a bank. Similarly, Itani et al. (2017) reported a positive association between B2B salespeople's adaptive selling behavior and their sales performance in a wide range of industries in India. Given the theoretical rationale and empirical evidence, this study posits that:

Hypothesis 4a: An export salesperson's adaptive selling behavior is positively related to his outcome performance.

Hypothesis 4b: An export salesperson's adaptive selling behavior is positively related to his relationship performance.

2.7.5 Salesperson's Customer-Qualification Skills and Salesperson's Performance

This study proposes that an export salesperson's customer-qualification skills and his sales performance are positively related. According to Sujan, Weitz, et al. (1988), the purpose of differentiating and categorizing customers is to reduce the complexity and difficulty of the selling proposition and communications. As salespeople with a high level of customer-qualification skills have a richer and clearly-defined knowledge structure about customer groups, they can effectively use the past knowledge to assess how much time and efforts should be invested in different types of customers and better understand which customers can flow through the sales funnel and result in a sale

(Ahearne et al., 2007; Sujan, et al., 1988). By doing so, a salesperson can spend more time and exert more sales efforts in establishing and building up good relationships with the most profitable customers and increasing his outcome performance(Järvinen & Taiminen, 2016). When a salesperson makes errors in customer qualification and fails to focus on the most profitable customers, such errors would result in wasted resources and losses in sales revenue (Järvinen & Taiminen, 2016; Monat, 2011). In addition, as salespeople with high customer-qualification skills have a better understanding about the characteristics of well-defined customer groups and can better predict customers' likely behavior based on their categorization knowledge, they are more likely to propose corresponding solutions or suggestions to satisfy customer needs and expectations (Román & Iacobucci, 2010). Despite scarce research investigating the impact of customer-qualification skills on salesperson relationship performance, the positive influence of customer-qualification skills on a salesperson's outcome performance is well established in personal selling (Román & Iacobucci, 2010; Román & Rodríguez, 2015; A. Sharma & Levy, 1995; A. Sharma et al., 2000; Sujan, et al., 1988). Based on these arguments, this study posits that:

Hypothesis 5a: An export salesperson's customer-qualification skills are positively associated with his outcome performance.

Hypothesis 5b: An export salesperson's customer-qualification skills are positively associated with his relationship performance.

2.7.6 Social Media Use in Sales and Salesperson's Performance

This study proposes that an export salesperson's social media use in sales will positively contribute to a salesperson's performance. Firstly, an export salesperson who can successfully integrate social media into his prospecting process can leverage great social networks via social media to "scout" a large pool of potential customers (Agnihotri et al., 2012). He can even ask friends, acquaintances, and even existing customers for more referrals. The great number of prospects based on social media anticipates more possibilities for a salesperson to increase outcome performance. Moreover, previous research shows that people's purchasing intention tends to be higher when they get the information from their friends or acquaintances (Dehghani & Tumer, 2015; Duffett, 2015). Therefore, export salespeople selling via social media may have more chances to close a deal. A survey of financial advisors reported those who used social media in sales expanded their client base by 21% and noted a 19% increase in revenue during the previous year (Rodriguez et al., 2013). Alarcón-del-Amo et al. (2015)'s empirical research also confirmed that exporters with more frequent social media use to interact with foreign customers reported better firm performance measured by perceived financial indicators than those with less social media use. Thus, this study posits that:

Hypothesis 6a: An export salesperson's social media use is positively related to his outcome performance.

Regarding customer relationship performance, this study argues that an export salesperson's social media use is conducive to the establishment and maintenance of customer relationships. Firstly, as social media allows anytime-anywhere communication access to both buyers and sellers, an export salesperson using social media can fully leverage this feature to overcome both the time and distance barriers to provide high-quality service such as increased responsiveness (Agnihotri et al., 2016), which helps improve customer relationship satisfaction and commitment (Agnihotri et al., 2016; N. Sharma & Patterson, 1999). Secondly, because social media is a platform for dynamic mutual communication, export salespeople who fully use social media in sales are more likely to listen to what customers say and make repeated real-time interactions with customers (Rodriguez et al., 2013). As a result, they build up trust and have a better understanding of each other, which are fundamental for the establishment and maintenance of customer relationships (Lacoste, 2016). In addition, export salespeople skillful at utilizing various functions of social media can present products information in a more diverse and vivid way to attract more prospects (Farrell & Hutasingh, 2018). The vivid presentation of product information is supposed to make interactions more acceptable and persuasive too, increasing the quality of communication (Andzulis et al., 2012). Communication of high quality (i.e. timely, helpful, easy, and pleasant) between a salesperson and a customer influences all facets of the relationship, especially in the aspects of trust, satisfaction, and loyalty (Ball et al., 2004). Additionally, the positive interpersonal interactions between export salespeople and customers on social media, like sending greetings for birthdays or special occasions, complement and facilitate business relationships as well (Agnihotri et al., 2012). In sum, this study argues that an export salesperson who can fully integrate social media into his sales processes can build up and maintain a better relationship with customers through his better listening to customers, high-quality service, interpersonal interactions, and repeated communication assisted by social media. The hypothesis is as follows.

Hypothesis 6b: An export salesperson's social media use is positively related to his relationship performance.

2.7.7 CQ and Salesperson's Customer-Qualification Skills

This study proposes that an export salesperson's CQ is positively associated with his customer-qualification skills. Hansen et al. (2011) argued that because salespeople with a high level of CQ have richer and more clearly defined hierarchical structures of cultural categories, they have advanced cognitive categorization capabilities to identify similarities and differences across countries. Following this logic, this study holds that salespeople with a high level of CQ tend to have higher customer-qualification skills due to their richer and more clearly defined hierarchical knowledge structures about foreign customers' needs, expectations, beliefs, norms, habits, preferences, etc. Moreover, because salespeople with a high level of CQ can better become aware of similarities and differences between cultures, they are more likely to classify foreign customers correctly according to their understanding of these similarities and differences (R. Brislin et al., 2006). In addition, since individuals high in CQ have a greater interest in knowing differences between countries, they may be more effective in identifying foreign customers' needs and expectations (Chen et al., 2012), which helps them qualify and classify customers as well. Based on these arguments, this study proposes that:

Hypothesis 7: An export salesperson's CQ is positively associated with his customer-qualification skills.

2.7.8 CQ and Adaptive Selling Behaviors

This study proposes a positive association between CQ and adaptive selling behaviors. This study draws on the adaptation theory and regards CQ as an export salesperson's characteristics to propose CQ as an antecedent of adaptive selling behavior. This study holds that CQ fits the knowledge dimension of a salesperson's characteristics to function as the antecedent of adaptive selling behavior. Drawing on the adaptation theory, this study argues that an export salesperson with a high level of CQ is equipped with a more relevant knowledge structure needed to practice adaptive selling behaviors and is motivated to commit more efforts to do so. According to Weitz et al. (1986), a salesperson needs an elaborate knowledge structure about the sales situations and customers to effectively practice adaptive selling behaviors. Ang et al. (2008)'s research shows that CQ reflects a person's level of cultural knowledge, which includes the norms, practices, and conventions in different cultures. Thus, an export salesperson with a high level of CQ is supposed to know more about the economic, legal, business, and interpersonal framework of the importing country and have a better understanding about the importer's business environment, beliefs, practices, communication styles, etc. In this way, CQ is supposed to serve as a part of the knowledge structure required to practice the adaptive selling behavior. A salesperson with a high level of CQ can leverage his intercultural knowledge structure to better adjust his presentation manners and content to communicate with foreign customers. Further, CQ reflects a salesperson's awareness of cultural similarities and differences between export and import countries, represents his motivation to change his selling behavior according to his assessment of customer's reactions during interactions and can transform this motivation into action, making the alteration of sales behaviors during interactions possible (Chen et al., 2012). Hansen et al. (2011) argued that salespeople with a high level of CQ are likely to be more effective in intercultural selling because they can better adapt to foreign customers' cultural backgrounds. Past research findings show that people with a high level of CQ tend to have more adaptive abilities (Charoensukmongkol, 2015a) and make more adjustments to their behaviors and communication styles during their cross-cultural communication (Ang et al., 2007; Oolders et al., 2008; Lin, Chen, & Song, 2012; Chen et al., 2014). Recently, Pandey and Charoensukmongkol (2019)'s research confirmed that export salespeople's CQ positively affects their adaptive selling behaviors in international trade shows. Aligning with previous research findings, this study argues that the higher level of CQ an export salesperson has, the more likely he will adjust their communication methods and change his selling behaviors during his interactions with customers in another country. To put it formally, this study proposes that:

Hypothesis 8: There is a positive association between an export salesperson's CQ and his adaptive selling behaviors.

2.7.9 CQ and Salesperson's Performance

This study proposes that an export salesperson's CQ is positively associated with his performance. Given that CQ has been identified as a critical cross-cultural competency to impact the effectiveness of cross-cultural interactions, it is supposed to influence the effectiveness of export selling as well (Pandey & Charoensukmongkol, 2019). Firstly, a salesperson with a high level of CQ is equipped with more cultural knowledge and awareness of similarities and differences in foreign markets, business practices, purchasing habits, consumption preferences, etc., which are necessary and fundamental information required for export selling (Hansen et al., 2011). A salesperson without such information will find it difficult to have effective interactions with foreign buyers (Hansen et al., 2011). Secondly, as Ang et al. (2007) and Chen et al. (2012) found, an individual with a high level of CQ tends to have stronger intercultural intrinsic motivation (i.e. intrinsic interest in foreign cultures) and intercultural self-efficacy (i.e. beliefs in one's intercultural effectiveness). Thus, an export salesperson with a high level of CQ tends to show stronger interest in getting to know about foreign buyers and markets, and more intrinsic motivations to exert more efforts, persistence, and resilience in face of intercultural barriers, and have more self-confidence in achieving superior performance in cross-cultural situations (Chen, Kirkman, Kim, Farh, & Tangirala, 2010; Chen et al., 2012; Ng et al., 2009). Imai and Gelfand (2010) found that in intercultural negotiation, people with a high level of CQ have more cooperative motives and commit more efforts to understand their culturally unfamiliar counterparts. Their research also concluded that CQ is a predictor of effectiveness in intercultural negotiation. Similarly, Shapiro, Ozanne, and Saatcioglu (2008) observed that when export managers are culturally sensitive to foreign customers, they negotiate more efficiently and are more successful in making trade deals. Previous empirical research has provided evidence supporting the positive association between CQ and salesperson's outcome performance in intercultural settings (Chen et al., 2012). Chen et al. (2012)'s research found that in intercultural sales (realtors and customers coming from different cultures), the realtors in U.S. real estate firms with a high level of motivational CQ have more sales transactions. Therefore, this study proposes that:

Hypothesis 9a: An export salesperson's CQ is positively related to his outcome performance.

Regarding the relationship between CQ and salesperson relationship performance, Charoensukmongkol (2015a) argued that CQ is a critical competency of SME exporters to develop good relationships with foreign customers and other foreign partners. The underlying reasons are threefold. Firstly, an export salesperson with a high level of CQ can better understand and satisfy foreign customers' expectations and needs due to their good cultural knowledge about importing countries and foreign people such as business practices, beliefs, purchasing preferences, etc. (Hansen et al., 2011). Given the higher possibility of developing good relationships with satisfied customers (Agnihotri et al., 2016), export salespeople with a high level of CQ tend to develop a better relationship with foreign customers. Secondly, export salespeople's appropriate cultural knowledge represented by CQ helps improve the quality of communication which is an important factor impacting the quality of relationships between business partners (Bstieler & Hemmert, 2008). An export salesperson with a high level of CQ can understand differences in foreign customers' communication styles and communicate in an appropriate way that makes customers feel more comfortable and friendlier, beneficial for the establishment and maintenance of customer relationships(Hansen et al., 2011). Thirdly, due to differences in attitudes, beliefs, values, and expectations, relationship-building and maintaining across cultures is more challenging than that within the same culture (Rockstuhl & Ng, 2008). Salespeople with a high level of CQ show stronger motivations and exert more efforts to cope with these challenges and adversity in export selling (Charoensukmongkol, 2015a). Their persistent commitment and appropriate behaviors positively affect their credibility perceived by foreign partners (Charoensukmongkol, 2015a). Such trust is significant for the establishment and maintenance of good relationships between exporters and importers. Literature has offered empirical evidence supporting the positive association between exporters' CQ and high-quality relationships with foreign customers (Charoensukmongkol, 2015a). By studying SME export companies in Thailand, Charoensukmongkol (2015a) found that SME export entrepreneurs' CQ is positively associated with the quality of the relationships SMEs develop with foreign customers, foreign suppliers, and foreign competitors. Therefore, this study argues that the higher level an export salesperson's CQ is in, the better relationship performance he will achieve. The hypothesis is presented as follows:

Hypothesis 9b: An export salesperson's CQ is positively related to his relationship performance.

The summary of research hypotheses and the conceptual model in this study are shown in Table 2.4 and Figure 2.4 respectively.

Table 2.4 Summary of Research Hypotheses

	Hypothesis
H1	An export salesperson's social media use in sales is positively associated with his customer-qualification skills
H2	An export salesperson's customer-qualification skills are positively associated with his adaptive selling behaviors
H3	There is a positive association between an export salesperson's social media use in sales and his adaptive selling behaviors

Continued

	Hypothesis
H4a	An export salesperson's adaptive selling behavior is positively related to his outcome performance
H4b	An export salesperson's adaptive selling behavior is positively related to his relationship performance
H5a	An export salesperson's customer-qualification skills are positively associated with his outcome performance
H5b	An export salesperson's customer-qualification skills are positively associated with his relationship performance
H6a	An export salesperson's social media use in sales is positively related to his outcome performance
H6b	An export salesperson's social media use in sales is positively related to his relationship performance
H7	An export salesperson's CQ is positively associated with his customer-qualification skills
H8	There is a positive association between an export salesperson's CQ and his adaptive selling behaviors
H9a	An export salesperson's CQ is positively related to his outcome performance
H9b	An export salesperson's CQ is positively related to his relationship performance

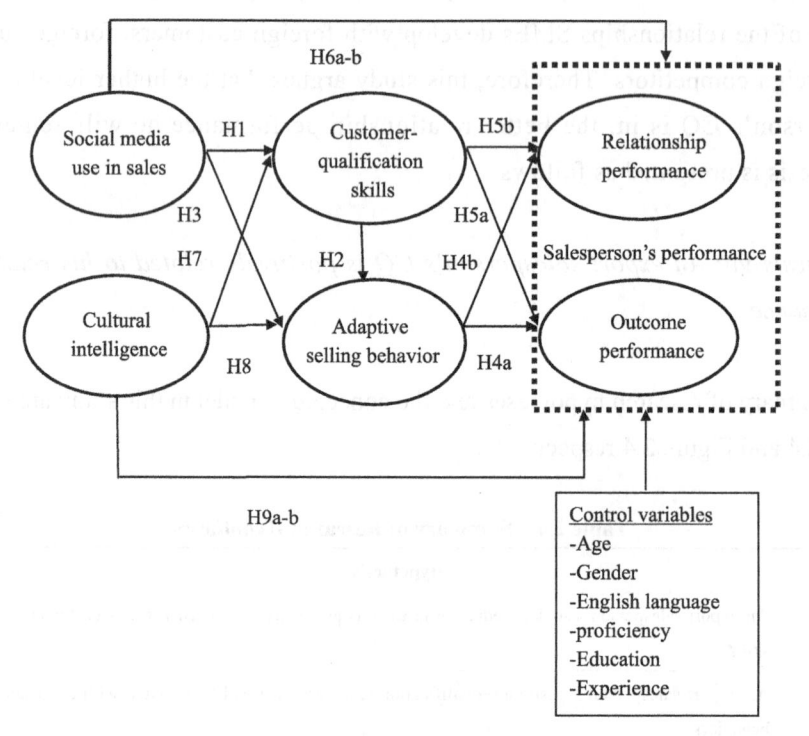

Figure 2.4 The Conceptual Model

CHAPTER 3　METHODOLOGY

3.1　Research Context

This study focuses on Chinese export salespeople who use social media in their selling processes. As an emerging country, China has experienced rapid economic growth since its accession to World Trade Organization (WTO) in December 2001. According to WTO (2015), China's export value in 2000 was about 250 billion U.S. dollars and ranked eleventh in the world. After its accession to WTO, China overtook Japan as the leading Asian exporter in 2004, surpassed the United States in 2007 and Germany in 2009 to become the world's leading exporter. In 2018, China's export value reached 2487 billion U.S. dollars (China Customs, 2019) and has ranked the first leading exporter in world merchandise trade for more than a decade (WTO, 2015).

The target population of this study is Chinese export salespeople who use social media in their export sales. Chinese export salespeople are a suitable population for this study because they use social media to assist in performing their export sales activities like finding new prospects, approaching, real-time communication with foreign buyers and online sales presentations, etc.(Wang et al., 2016). They cater to foreign buyers' preferences for social media use and make appropriate choices in social media Apps (Wang et al., 2016). Given the large population of Chinese export salespeople and their use of social media in export sales, Chinese export salespeople are the ideal research population for this study.

3.2 Sample Selection

The sample of this study will be selected using probability methods. In probability sampling, the sample is selected based on randomization and every unit in the population has an equal, known, and nonzero probability of being selected (Gary, 1990). Due to its random selection procedure, the probability sampling technique is regarded as the most efficient sampling methodology and the results of the studies based on this sampling technique can be generalized to the target population (Acharya et al., 2013). In this study, the sampling frame of research is the list of export salespeople provided on the FOB business Forum website. The website was built by FOB Shanghai Company in 2000 and aimed to offer a platform for foreign trade practitioners to share information and knowledge about international trade. Up to now, the website has 2,631,535 registered members and boasts as the largest professional web portal for Chinese export and import practitioners. From January to December in 2018, the average number of monthly new posts uploaded to the website was 139,540 and about 8,000 members visited the website daily (FOB Shanghai, 2019). Interested members can join their virtual communities like inspection community, logistics community, import community, export community, exhibition community, etc. Members publicize their name cards which include contact information like username, email, company name, location (city), and telephone number. As this study targets on export salespeople, the author focuses on the export community on the FOB business Forum website. There are 83,100 publicized name cards in total in the export community and the author collected 24,191 export salesperson's information with full contact information. The collected information shows that 24,191 export salespeople in the database come from 24,177 export companies specializing in 22 fields including textiles, clothing and accessories and, toys, etc. These 24,191 export salespeople from the FOB business Forum website constitute the sampling frame of this study. Figure 3.1 shows the distribution of reachable export salespeople in trade fields.

CHAPTER 3 METHODOLOGY

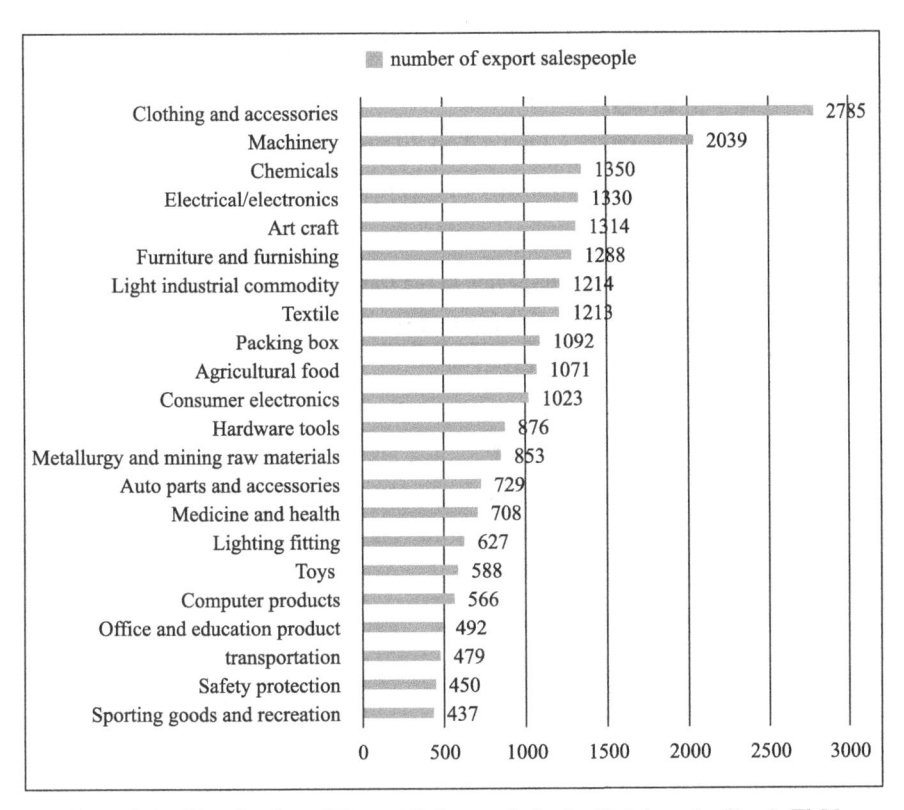

Trade field	Number of export salespeople
Clothing and accessories	2785
Machinery	2039
Chemicals	1350
Electrical/electronics	1330
Art craft	1314
Furniture and furnishing	1288
Light industrial commodity	1214
Textile	1213
Packing box	1092
Agricultural food	1071
Consumer electronics	1023
Hardware tools	876
Metallurgy and mining raw materials	853
Auto parts and accessories	729
Medicine and health	708
Lighting fitting	627
Toys	588
Computer products	566
Office and education product	492
transportation	479
Safety protection	450
Sporting goods and recreation	437

Figure 3.1 Distribution of Export Salespeople in the Database by Trade Fields

To ensure the representativeness of the accessible export salespeople, the researcher analyzed the location of these salespeople. Preliminary analysis shows that 95.94% of reachable export salespeople in the database are located in Chinese top 20 provinces and municipalities in terms of export value. The export value of the top 20 provinces and municipalities accounts for 97.76% of total Chinese export value in 2018(China Customs, 2019). Table 3.1 presents the China's top 20 provinces and municipalities ranked by export value (China Customs, 2019) and the distribution of reachable export salespeople in these areas. According to Table 3.1, the top 20 provinces and municipalities where the reachable export companies are located are almost the same as Chinese top 20 provinces and municipalities ranked by export value (except for the last one Xinjiang) and their distribution patterns are quite similar except for minor variances in three provinces (Jiangsu, Zhejiang, Hebei). The number of reachable export salespeople in Zhejiang is strikingly higher than that in Jiangsu (see Figure 3.2). And the percentage of reachable export salespeople in Hebei (3.75%) is much higher than that of its export value in the whole country. Despite these variances, the locations of 95.94% reachable export salespeople in the database cover China's Top 20 provinces and municipalities by export value, which increases the generalizability of this research.

Table 3.1　Distribution of Export Salespeople in the Database in China's Top 20 Provinces and Municipalities by Export Value

Provinces and municipalities	Export value		Salespeople	
	USD	Percentage	Number	Percentage
Guangdong	646593896545.00	26.59%	7361	30.43%
Jiangsu	404014507134.00	16.24%	2198	9.09%
Zhejiang	321135962836.00	12.91%	5326	22.02%
Shanghai	207159967483.00	8.33%	1704	7.04%
Shandong	160127555499.00	6.44%	1805	7.46%
Fujian	115549506708.00	4.65%	1351	5.58%
Beijing	74105752991.00	2.98%	550	2.27%
Henan	53777606637.00	2.16%	271	1.12%
Chongqing	51355665606.00	2.06%	108	0.45%
Sichuan	50395173712.00	2.03%	144	0.60%
Tianjin	48813085236.00	1.96%	307	1.27%
Liaoning	48795406504.00	1.96%	210	0.87%
Anhui	36198026539.00	1.46%	231	0.95%
Hubei	34082623166.00	1.37%	244	1.01%
Hebei	33980535582.00	1.37%	906	3.75%
Jiangxi	33942676483.00	1.36%	104	0.43%
Guangxi	32791439127.00	1.32%	92	0.38%
Shaanxi	31595241708.00	1.27%	144	0.60%
Hunan	30539034324.00	1.23%	153	0.63%
Xinjiang	16413060302.00	0.66%	0	0.00%
Total	2431366724122.00	97.76%	23209	95.94%
Total export value in China	2487043528112.00		24191	
24191=total number of export companies in the database			
export value from China Customs (2019)			

CHAPTER 3   METHODOLOGY

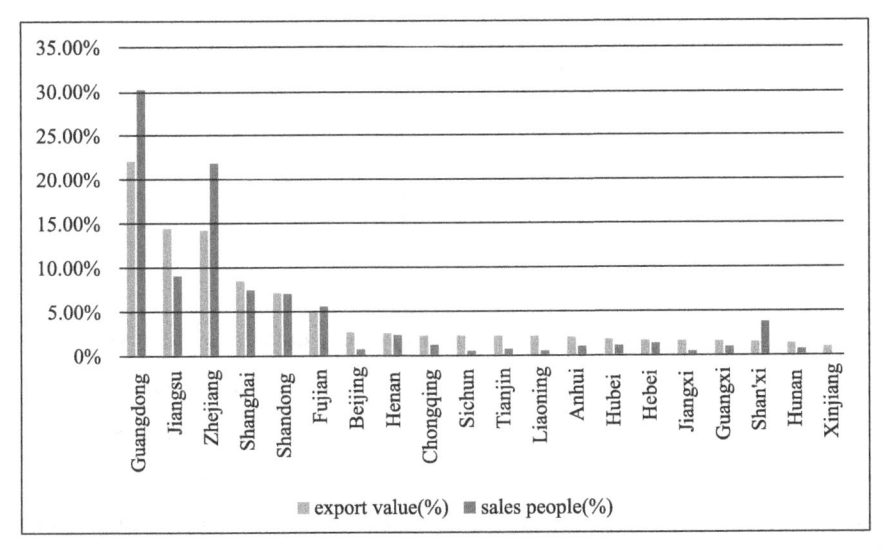

Figure 3.2   A Comparison of the Percentage of Export Value and that of Export Salespeople in the Database in China's Top 20 Provinces and Municipalities by Export Value

3.3   Data Collection Method

Due to the limitation in time and resources, this study adopts a questionnaire survey method as the data collection method because this method allows researchers to collect information from a large number of respondents in a short period of time (Bell et al., 2018). To ensure the validity and reliability of the research, the survey guarantees the anonymity and the use of data for only academic purposes to encourage the respondents to respond truthfully to the questionnaires (Bell et al., 2018). The questionnaire will be distributed in an online form via Wenjuanxing, a Chinese professional survey website popular for its expertise in helping researchers and marketers make surveys (Liu et al., 2016; Zheng & Zheng, 2014). The author will send an email to every individual export salesperson in the database. The email contains a cover letter explaining the purpose of the research and a link to the online questionnaire. The respondents can also scan the QR code in the letter and finish the questionnaire on their mobile phones as well. As a token of gratitude, the author will offer monetary incentives for each sincere participant. Each participant who finishes the questionnaire in a reasonable time will receive one dollar through the survey website. This practice has been adopted by prior researchers collecting data in China (Ou et al., 2014).

3.4 Questionnaire Development

This study uses a structured questionnaire to collect data. All the scales measuring dependent and independent variables are adopted from prior studies. Using existing scales to collect data in a study has several advantages. Firstly, because the existing scales have been tested for the first time, they are regarded as good indicators of the measured concepts (Hyman et al., 2006). Moreover, because the existing scales have been repeatedly tested by other researchers, their reliability and validity and the quality of data tend to be high (Hyman et al., 2006). Another advantage of using existing scales is that it is more cost-effective and time-saving than developing a new scale (Hyman et al., 2006). Lastly, the use of existing scales also makes the comparison of the research findings with other scholars' findings possible (Meadows, 2003).

As most of the scales used in the study are in English (except for an existing Chinese version of CQ scale), this study adopts translation and back-translation methods to develop the questionnaire in Chinese. Scholars suggest that translation and backtranslation are the most commonly used methods to ensure the quality and validity of instruments in different languages (R. W. Brislin, 1970; Sperber, 2004). The questionnaire is first compiled in English under the instruction of the advisor, translated into Chinese and then back-translated by a professional translator to ensure the validity of the questionnaire (Hult et al., 2008).

Scholars argued that a pilot test is crucial for a good research design because it may offer advance warning about where the study may fail or help identify the inappropriate, ambiguous, or too complicated instruments (De Vaus, 2013; Van Teijlingen & Hundley, 2001). The author will discuss the content of the questionnaire with three export salespeople and make minor adjustments to ensure the conciseness and clarity of the wording of the questionnaire. A pilot test will be conducted with a small number of respondents (Clark & Watson, 1995).

3.5 Measurement

All the items in the questionnaire to measure dependent variables and independent variables are developed from the existing literature. The measurement of each construct is presented in detail in the following part.

3.5.1 Social Media Use in Sales

This study follows Moore et al. (2015)'s practices to measure social media use in sales. The construct is operationalized as the frequency a salesperson uses social media for each stage of the sales process, i.e. prospecting, preapproach, approach, sales presentation, handling objections, closing the sale, and follow-up service. Respondents are asked to state which type of social media is used for each stage and how often they use it for each stage. For the first part of each question, the questionnaire will offer a list of common social media Apps and ask the respondents to choose all social media they use for each stage and add the others they use if not included in the list. For the second part of each question, all the question items will be rated on a five-point Likert scale ranging from 1(never) to 5 (very often) and details are as follows.

(1) How often do you use social media for prospecting?
(2) How often do you use social media for preapproach?
(3) How often do you use social media for approach?
(4) How often do you use social media for sales presentation?
(5) How often do you use social media for handling objections?
(6) How often do you use social media for closing the deal?
(7) How often do you use social media for follow-up service?

3.5.2 Salesperson's Customer-Qualification Skills

The salesperson's customer-qualification skills are measured by a three-item scale developed by Román and Iacobucci (2010). Respondents are asked to rate themselves on five-point Likert-type items ranging from 1 (needs improvement) to 5 (outstanding). The reliability and validity of the scale has been confirmed in past research (Román & Iacobucci, 2010; Román & Rodríguez, 2015). All the question items are as follows.

(1) My ability to identify and analyze customer's needs is...
(2) My ability to understand the customer's buying motive is...
(3) My ability to distinguish different kinds of customers is...

3.5.3 Adaptive Selling Behaviors

Adaptive selling behaviors are measured by a five-item ADAPTS-SV scale (Robinson Jr et al., 2002). The validity and reliability of the scale has been confirmed in prior research (Chakrabarty et al., 2004; Chakrabarty et al., 2014; Guenzi et al., 2016). Respondents are asked to rate themselves on five-point Likert-type items ranging from 1 (strongly disagree) to 5 (strongly agree). All the question items are as follows.

(1) When I feel that my sales approach is not working, I can easily change to another approach.
(2) I like to experiment with different sales approaches.
(3) I am very flexible in the selling approach I use.
(4) I can easily use a wide range of selling approaches.
(5) I try to understand how one customer differs from another.

3.5.4 Salesperson's Performance

This study uses self-rated scales to measure a salesperson's performance. Salespeople's self-evaluations of their own performance have been extensively documented in sales literature (Babakus et al., 1999; Banin et al., 2016; Román & Iacobucci, 2010; Sujan et al., 1994; Verbeke & Bagozzi, 2000; Wachner et al., 2009). Scholars argued that salespeople are in the best position to judge their own performance because they have a good understanding of all the parts of their own sales job(Levy & Sharma, 1993; Román & Iacobucci, 2010). Kock (2017b)'s comparative analysis of self-reported job performance and official supervisor evaluations finds that using self-reported instruments to measure job performance shows good reliability and validity as well as low collinearity and may be better than supervisor evaluations measurement.

Following previous sales studies (Ogilvie et al., 2018; Rodriguez & Honeycutt Jr., 2011; Sundaram et al., 2007), this study focuses on two dimensions of salesperson's performance, which are salesperson's outcome performance and salesperson's customer relationship performance. The measurements are presented in detail in the following part.

3.5.4.1 Salesperson's outcome performance

Salesperson's outcome performance was measured by a four-item scale developed by Behrman and Perrault (1982). The respondents are asked to self-evaluate their sales performance in terms of selling high profit-margin products, generating a high level of dollar sales, quickly generating sales of new company products, and exceeding sales targets. All the items are scored by a five-point rating scale, ranging from 1(strongly negative) to 5 (strongly positive). All the question items to measure salesperson outcome performance are as follows.

Please indicate your opinions about your performance regarding.
(1) Selling high profit-margin products.
(2) Generating a high level of dollar sales.
(3) Quickly generating sales of new company products.
(4) Exceeding sales targets.

3.5.4.2 Salesperson's relationship performance

Salesperson relationship performance is measured by a three-item scale developed by Rodriguez et al. (2013). Rodriguez et al. (2013) developed the scale based on Hunter and Perreault Jr. (2007)'s relational measures of sales performance, which focus on behaviors that strengthen the relationship between buyers and sellers. Items are scored on a five-point Likert scale, ranging from 1 (strongly disagree) to 5 (strongly agree). All the items are as follows.

(1) Compared to last year, my new account acquisition has increased.
(2) Compared to last year, the number of my qualified opportunities/leads has increased.
(3) Compared to last year, my customer retention rate has increased.

3.5.5 Cultural Intelligence

Cultural intelligence is measured by a set of self-reported cultural intelligence scales developed by Ang et al. (2007). The scales have twenty items, six to measure cognitive CQ, four to measure meta-cognitive CQ, five to measure motivational CQ, and five to measure behavioral CQ. All items are measured by five-point Likert scales ranging from 1 (strongly disagree) to 5 (strongly agree). All the question items are as follows.

1. Metacognitive CQ
(1) I am conscious of the cultural knowledge I use when interacting with people with different cultural backgrounds.
(2) I adjust my cultural knowledge as I interact with people from a culture that is unfamiliar to me.
(3) I am conscious of the cultural knowledge I apply to cross-cultural interactions.
(4) I check the accuracy of my cultural knowledge as I interact with people from different cultures.
2. Cognitive CQ
(1) I know the legal and economic systems of other cultures.
(2) I know the rules (e.g. vocabulary, grammar) of other languages.

(3) I know the cultural values and religious beliefs of other cultures.
(4) I know the marriage systems of other cultures.
(5) I know the arts and crafts of other cultures.
(6) I know the rules for expressing non-verbal behaviors in other cultures.

3. Motivational CQ
(1) I enjoy interacting with people from different cultures.
(2) I am confident that I can socialize with locals in a culture that is unfamiliar to me.
(3) I am sure I can deal with the stresses of adjusting to a culture that is new to me.
(4) I enjoy living in cultures that are unfamiliar to me.
(5) I am confident that I can get accustomed to the shopping conditions in a different culture.

4. Behavioral CQ
(1) I change my verbal behavior (e.g. accent, tone) when a cross-cultural interaction requires it.
(2) I use pause and silence differently to suit different cross-cultural situations.
(3) I vary the rate of my speaking when a cross-cultural situation requires it.
(4) I change my non-verbal behavior when a cross-cultural situation requires it
(5) I alter my facial expressions when a cross-cultural interaction requires it.

3.6 Control Variables

According to the literature, this study includes five control variables that may influence the salesperson's outcome performance and relationship performance. The five control variables are gender, age, experience, education, and English language proficiency. They will be explained in detail as follows.

3.6.1 Gender

Literature suggests that the gender difference between male and female salespeople may influence salesperson performance (Swan & Futrell, 1978). Although many studies found no significant difference in the self-reported sales performance between male and female salespeople (Moncrief et al., 2000; Palmer & Bejou, 1995; Piercy et al., 2012; Siguaw & Honeycutt Jr., 1995; Wachner et al., 2009), there was a stereotype about women salespeople portrayed as poorer performers than men counterparts (Swan & Futrell, 1978). Swan and Futrell (1978)'s research findings showed that female salespeople had less product knowledge and technical ability, territory coverage, activity reporting, and overall performance. However, in terms of relationship performance, female salespeople may excel at developing ongoing relationships due to their female traits such as empathy (Palmer & Bejou, 1995), warm, nurturing, and supportive role (Siguaw & Honeycutt Jr., 1995) and their greater importance on social relationships than male counterparts (McNeilly & Goldsmith, 1991; Russ & McNeilly, 1995). Gender is measured by dummy variables, with females coded as 0 and males coded as 1.

3.6.2 Age

Previous research found that age and salesperson performance may be related (Landau & Werbel, 1995; Wachner et al., 2009). Ford, Walker Jr., Churchill Jr., and Hartley (1987)'s meta-analysis about factors influencing sales performance found that age explained a significant but small percentage of sales performance. Landau and Werbel (1995)'s research found that older new hires who use a variety of prospecting techniques tend to have higher sales productivity (measured by average monthly commissions for the first six months of employment). Older salespeople are more likely to have higher sales performance due to greater social networks (Landau & Werbel, 1995) and more sales experience in their industry (Wachner et al., 2009). This control variable is measured by a salesperson's actual age.

3.6.3 Experience

A salesperson's selling experience is a potentially important predictor of his sales performance (Bartkus et al., 1989; Walker Jr et al., 1977). The longer a salesperson works in an industry or field, the more chances he will meet various customers and complex encounters, the more knowledge and understanding he will have about customer types, sales skills, sales strategy, etc., which helps improve his sales performance and establish good relationships with customers (Johlke, 2006; Mintu-Wimsatt & Gassenheimer, 2004; Shoemaker & Johlke, 2002). Previous research findings noted that a salesperson with higher levels of selling experience tended to have higher levels of sales performance (Bartkus et al., 1989; Franke & Park, 2006; Pfeffer, 1985; Wachner et al., 2009). Experience is measured by the number of years a salesperson has worked as an export salesperson. Such a practice has been adopted by previous studies (Borman et al., 1993; Giacobbe et al., 2006; McDaniel et al., 1988; Schmidt et al., 1986).

3.6.4 Education

Education level can be a predictor of salesperson performance (Churchill Jr et al., 1985) because education develops people's critical thinking and abilities to deal with complex situations, which are necessary for a salesperson to fulfill his selling tasks (Levy & Sharma, 1994). Salespeople with a higher level of education can more easily acquire substantial product knowledge and are more capable of efficiently dealing with complex sales encounters than those with a lower one (Kotur & Anbazhagan, 2014). Past empirical research found that a salesperson's education level was positively associated with his sales performance (Cotham, 1969; Lamont & Lundstrom, 1977). This variable is measured by an ordinal scale (1= "high school/high vocational certificate", 2= "diploma", 3= "bachelor's degree", 4= "master's degree and above").

3.6.5 English Language Proficiency

In export selling, salespeople's foreign language competence may influence their communication with foreign buyers and their sales performance (Enderwick & Akoorie, 1994; Enderwick & Gray, 1993). A Higher level of foreign language competence is helpful for smooth communication whereas lower levels may impede communication during interactions or negotiations with foreign customers, which is not conducive to closing a deal(Clarke, 1999; Crick, 1999). As most Chinese export salespeople use

English to communicate with importers, this study mainly takes their English language proficiency into consideration for the convenience of comparison. Chinese export salespeople's English language proficiency is measured by an ordinal scale (1= "less than College English Test Band 4"; 2= "College English Test Band 4", 3= "College English Test 6 or Test for English Majors Band 4"; 4= "Test for English Majors Band 8 or above"). In China, the College English Test (CET) and Test for English Majors (TEM) are two major and common tests for English Levels. CET bands consist of Band 4 and Band 6, and TEM bands include Band 4 and Band 8. For both CET and TEM, the bigger band number suggests a higher level of English proficiency. Usually, the level of CET Band 6 is regarded as the same level as TEM Band 4.

3.7 Data Processing Tools and Analysis

This study will use the Partial Least Squares Structural Equation Modeling (PLS-SEM) approach to analyze data and estimate the proposed model. PLS-SEM is a representative of the variance-based least squares estimation technique (Chin et al., 2003; Vinzi et al., 2010). Its primary objective is to make causal-predictive analysis of data high in complexity but low in theoretical support (Henseler, Ringle, & Sinkovics, 2009). In recent years, PLS-SEM has been widely adopted for data analysis in business research fields such as accounting (L. Lee et al., 2011), operations management (Peng & Lai, 2012), marketing (Hair et al., 2012), human resources management (Charoensukmongkol et al., 2013, 2015; Charoensukmongkol & Suthatorn, 2018; Koirala & Charoensukmongkol, 2018; Phungsoonthorn & Charoensukmongkol, 2018; Puyod & Charoensukmongkol, 2019b), psychology (Charoensukmongkol, 2015b, 2016b, 2016d, 2017, 2019a, 2019c, 2019d; Charoensukmongkol & Aumeboonsuke, 2017; Charoensukmongkol et al., 2016; Nongpong & Charoensukmongkol, 2016) and strategic management (Charoensukmongkol, 2016c; Hair et al., 2012; Hair et al., 2014; Tanchaitranon & Charoensukmongkol, 2016). The wide popularity of PLS-SEM among researchers is mainly due to its following characteristics: prediction-oriented, small sample size, non-normal distribution, formative measurement models, and complex models (Hair et al., 2011; Hair et al., 2014; Henseler et al., 2009).

This study adopts the PLS-SEM approach for the data analysis mainly for the following reasons. Firstly, Hair et al. (2014) suggested that PLS-SEM is a suitable method for analyzing data with a multivariate non-normal distribution. This advantage of PLS-SEM matches with the nature of the data in this study which is likely to be non-normally distributed. Scholars like Peng and Lai (2012) and Hair et al. (2014) have pointed out that data collected in social science research often follow a multivariate non-normal distribution. Secondly, Rigdon, Sarstedt, and Ringle (2017) suggested that PLS-SEM is suitable for exploratory research with low theoretical support and a lack of clear determination of the applicable measurement models. This advantage of PLS-SEM matches with this study's research objectives, which are to some extent exploratory in nature. This study aims to predict the variance of dependent variables from a set of independent variables, and the relationships between social media use in sales and customer-qualification skills, CQ and customer-qualification skills, customer-qualification skills and salesperson relationship performance have not been previously explored. Thirdly, Chin (2010) argued that PLS-SEM is advantageous in analyzing complex models with a high number of indicators and constructs. Such an advantage of PLS-SEM matches with the complexity of the proposed model in this study. This study has six constructs and proposed thirteen hypotheses in total. In addition, the CQ construct consists of four dimensions measured by twenty indicators. Considering all these factors, this study adopts PLS-SEM for its data analysis. As for the data processing tools, this study will use WarpPLS version 6.0 software to make data analysis (Kock, 2017a).

APPENDICES

Appendix A Questionnaire (English)

This survey is conducted on a voluntary basis and conducted for academic purposes only. You can choose not to participate in the study. The information gathered in this survey is confidential and does not involve any leakage of your privacy. The answers will only be processed as statistical observations. All the questions in this survey only indicate your opinions about them and do not have any right or wrong answers. You can skip answering any questions that you feel uncomfortable to answer.

Part I: Demographics

1. Gender:
    □ [1] Male   □ [2] Female

2. Age:
    _____ years old

3. Work experiences in export sales:
    □ [1] less than 1 year
    □ [2] 1–5 years
    □ [3] 6–10 years
    □ [4] more than 10 years

4. Workplace (Please specify the city):

_____

5. Education:
   - □ ¹ high school/high vocational certificate
   - □ ² diploma
   - □ ³ bachelor's degree
   - □ ⁴ master's degree and above

6. Monthly salary:
   - □ ¹ below 5000 RMB
   - □ ² 5001–8000 RMB
   - □ ³ 8001–12000 RMB
   - □ ⁴ 12001 RMB or above

7. English language proficiency:
   - □ ¹ less than College English Test Band 4
   - □ ² College English Test Band 4
   - □ ³ College English Test Band 6/ Test for English Majors Band 4
   - □ ⁴ Test for English Majors Band 8 or above

8. Job title:
   - □ ¹ sales representative   □ ² sales manager   □ ³ general sales manager

9. Customer type:
   - □ ¹ B2B   □ ² B2C   □ ³ both B2B and B2C

10. Targeted country (Please specify countries you sell goods/provide services in a sequence of sales value from the most to the least; no more than three countries):

    _____

11. Trade industry:
    - □ ¹ industrial goods   □ ² consumer goods

Part II: Questions for Social Media Use in Sales

Please specify all the social media you use in the following seven processes and the frequency you use them.

Social Media Use in Chinese Export Sales
社交媒体在中国出口销售中的应用

1A. Please choose all the social media you use for **prospecting** and add the others you use if not included in the list.

Facebook	YouTube	WhatsApp	Facebook Messenger	WeChat
Skype	QQ	Q zone	LinkedIn	Instagram
Reddit	Twitter	Vkontakte	TikTok	Sina Weibo
Vimeo	Snapchat	Viber+	Pinterest	LINE
Karao Talk	Google+	Tumblr		

1B. How often do you use the social media you indicate in the above for **prospecting**?

☐ [1] never ☐ [2] rarely ☐ [3] sometimes ☐ [4] often ☐ [5] very often

2A. Please choose all social media you use for **preapproach** and add the others you use if not included in the list.

Facebook	YouTube	WhatsApp	Facebook Messenger	WeChat
Skype	QQ	Q zone	LinkedIn	Instagram
Reddit	Twitter	Vkontakte	TikTok	Sina Weibo
Vimeo	Snapchat	Viber+	Pinterest	LINE
Karao Talk	Google+	Tumblr		

2B. How often do you use the social media you indicate in the above for **preapproach**?

☐ ¹never ☐ ²rarely ☐ ³sometimes ☐ ⁴often ☐ ⁵very often

3A. Please choose all the social media you use for **approach** and add the others you use if not included in the list.

Facebook	YouTube	WhatsApp	Facebook Messenger	WeChat
Skype	QQ	Q zone	LinkedIn	Instagram
Reddit	Twitter	Vkontakte	TikTok	Sina Weibo
Vimeo	Snapchat	Viber+	Pinterest	LINE
Karao Talk	Google+	Tumblr		

3B. How often do you use the social media you indicate in the above for **approach**?

☐ ¹never ☐ ²rarely ☐ ³sometimes ☐ ⁴often ☐ ⁵very often

4A. Please choose all the social media you use for **sales presentation** and add the others you use if not included in the list.

Facebook	YouTube	WhatsApp	Facebook Messenger	WeChat
Skype	QQ	Q zone	LinkedIn	Instagram

Reddit	Twitter	Vkontakte	TikTok	Sina Weibo
Vimeo	Snapchat	Viber+	Pinterest	LINE
Karao Talk	Google+	Tumblr		

4B. How often do you use the social media you indicate in the above for **sales presentation**?

☐ ¹ never ☐ ² rarely ☐ ³ sometimes ☐ ⁴ often ☐ ⁵ very often

5A. Please choose all the social media you use for **handling objections** and add the others you use if not included in the list.

Facebook	YouTube	WhatsApp	Facebook Messenger	WeChat
Skype	QQ	Q zone	LinkedIn	Instagram
Reddit	Twitter	Vkontakte	TikTok	Sina Weibo
Vimeo	Snapchat	Viber+	Pinterest	LINE
Karao Talk	Google+	Tumblr		

5B. How often do you use the social media you indicate in the above for **handling objections**?

☐ ¹ never ☐ ² rarely ☐ ³ sometimes ☐ ⁴ often ☐ ⁵ very often

6A. Please choose all the social media you use for **closing the deal** and add the others you use if not included in the list.

Facebook	YouTube	WhatsApp	Facebook Messenger	WeChat
Skype	QQ	Q zone	LinkedIn	Instagram
Reddit	Twitter	Vkontakte	TikTok	Sina Weibo
Vimeo	Snapchat	Viber+	Pinterest	LINE
Karao Talk	Google+	Tumblr		

6B. How often do you use the social media you indicate in the above for **closing the deal**?

☐ [1] never ☐ [2] rarely ☐ [3] sometimes ☐ [4] often ☐ [5] very often

7A. Please choose all the social media you use for **follow-up service** and add the others you use if not included in the list.

Facebook	YouTube	WhatsApp	Facebook Messenger	WeChat
Skype	QQ	Q zone	LinkedIn	Instagram
Reddit	Twitter	Vkontakte	TikTok	Sina Weibo

Vimeo	Snapchat	Viber+	Pinterest	LINE
Karao Talk	Google+	Tumblr		

7B. How often do you use the social media you indicate in the above for **follow-up service**?

☐ ¹ never ☐ ² rarely ☐ ³ sometimes ☐ ⁴ often ☐ ⁵ very often

Part III: Questions for Salesperson's Customer Qualification Skills

Please rate yourself in terms of the following statements by items ranging from 1 (needs improvement) to 5 (excellent).

8. My ability to identify and analyze customers' needs is:
   ☐ ¹ needs improvement ☐ ² fair ☐ ³ good ☐ ⁴ excellent
   ☐ ⁵ outstanding

9. My ability to understand customers' buying motive is:
   ☐ ¹ needs improvement ☐ ² fair ☐ ³ good ☐ ⁴ excellent
   ☐ ⁵ outstanding

10. My ability to distinguish different kinds of customers is:
    ☐ ¹ needs improvement ☐ ² fair ☐ ³ good ☐ ⁴ excellent
    ☐ ⁵ outstanding

Part IV: Questions for Adaptive Selling Behaviors

Please specify your opinions of agreement or disagreement about the following statements.

11. When I feel that my sales approach is not working, I can easily change to another approach.

☐ ¹ strongly disagree ☐ ² disagree ☐ ³ neutral ☐ ⁴ agree
☐ ⁵ strongly agree

12. I like to experiment with different sales approaches.
    ☐ ¹ strongly disagree ☐ ² disagree ☐ ³ neutral ☐ ⁴ agree
    ☐ ⁵ strongly agree

13. I am very flexible in the selling approach I use.
    ☐ ¹ strongly disagree ☐ ² disagree ☐ ³ neutral ☐ ⁴ agree
    ☐ ⁵ strongly agree

14. I can easily use a wide range of selling approaches.
    ☐ ¹ strongly disagree ☐ ² disagree ☐ ³ neutral ☐ ⁴ agree
    ☐ ⁵ strongly agree

15. I try to understand how one customer differs from another.
    ☐ ¹ strongly disagree ☐ ² disagree ☐ ³ neutral ☐ ⁴ agree
    ☐ ⁵ strongly agree

Part V: Questions for Salesperson's Performance

Please indicate your opinions about your performance regarding.

16. Selling high profit–margin products:
    ☐ ¹ needs improvement ☐ ² fair ☐ ³ good ☐ ⁴ excellent
    ☐ ⁵ outstanding

17. Generating a high level of dollar sales:
    ☐ ¹ needs improvement ☐ ² fair ☐ ³ good ☐ ⁴ excellent
    ☐ ⁵ outstanding

18. Quickly generating sales of new company products:
    ☐ ¹ needs improvement ☐ ² fair ☐ ³ good ☐ ⁴ excellent
    ☐ ⁵ outstanding

19. Exceeding sales targets:
    - ☐ ¹ needs improvement
    - ☐ ² fair
    - ☐ ³ good
    - ☐ ⁴ excellent
    - ☐ ⁵ outstanding

Please specify your opinions of agreement or disagreement about the following statements.

20. Compared to last year, new account acquisition has increased.
    - ☐ ¹ strongly disagree
    - ☐ ² disagree
    - ☐ ³ neutral
    - ☐ ⁴ agree
    - ☐ ⁵ strongly agree

21. Compared to last year, the number of qualified opportunities/leads has increased.
    - ☐ ¹ strongly disagree
    - ☐ ² disagree
    - ☐ ³ neutral
    - ☐ ⁴ agree
    - ☐ ⁵ strongly agree

22. Compared to last year, my customer retention rate has increased.
    - ☐ ¹ strongly disagree
    - ☐ ² disagree
    - ☐ ³ neutral
    - ☐ ⁴ agree
    - ☐ ⁵ strongly agree

Part VI: Questions for Cultural Intelligence

Please specify your opinions of agreement or disagreement about the following statements.

23. I am conscious of the cultural knowledge I use when interacting with people with different cultural backgrounds.
    - ☐ ¹ strongly disagree
    - ☐ ² disagree
    - ☐ ³ neutral
    - ☐ ⁴ agree
    - ☐ ⁵ strongly agree

24. I adjust my cultural knowledge as I interact with people from a culture that is unfamiliar to me.
    - ☐ ¹ strongly disagree
    - ☐ ² disagree
    - ☐ ³ neutral
    - ☐ ⁴ agree
    - ☐ ⁵ strongly agree

25. I am conscious of the cultural knowledge I apply to cross-cultural interactions.
    - ☐ ¹ strongly disagree
    - ☐ ² disagree
    - ☐ ³ neutral
    - ☐ ⁴ agree
    - ☐ ⁵ strongly agree

26. I check the accuracy of my cultural knowledge as I interact with people from different cultures.
    - ☐ ¹ strongly disagree
    - ☐ ² disagree
    - ☐ ³ neutral
    - ☐ ⁴ agree
    - ☐ ⁵ strongly agree

27. I know the legal and economic systems of other countries.
    - ☐ ¹ strongly disagree
    - ☐ ² disagree
    - ☐ ³ neutral
    - ☐ ⁴ agree
    - ☐ ⁵ strongly agree

28. I know the rules (e.g. vocabulary, grammar) of other languages.
    - ☐ ¹ strongly disagree
    - ☐ ² disagree
    - ☐ ³ neutral
    - ☐ ⁴ agree
    - ☐ ⁵ strongly agree

29. I know the cultural values and religious beliefs of other cultures.
    - ☐ ¹ strongly disagree
    - ☐ ² disagree
    - ☐ ³ neutral
    - ☐ ⁴ agree
    - ☐ ⁵ strongly agree

30. I know the marriage systems of other cultures.
    - ☐ ¹ strongly disagree
    - ☐ ² disagree
    - ☐ ³ neutral
    - ☐ ⁴ agree
    - ☐ ⁵ strongly agree

31. I know the arts and crafts of other cultures.
    - ☐ ¹ strongly disagree
    - ☐ ² disagree
    - ☐ ³ neutral
    - ☐ ⁴ agree
    - ☐ ⁵ strongly agree

32. I know the rules for expressing non-verbal behaviors in other cultures.
    - ☐ ¹ strongly disagree
    - ☐ ² disagree
    - ☐ ³ neutral
    - ☐ ⁴ agree
    - ☐ ⁵ strongly agree

33. I enjoy interacting with people from different cultures.
    ☐ ¹ strongly disagree　　☐ ² disagree　　☐ ³ neutral　　☐ ⁴ agree
    ☐ ⁵ strongly agree

34. I am confident that I can socialize with locals in a culture that is unfamiliar to me.
    ☐ ¹ strongly disagree　　☐ ² disagree　　☐ ³ neutral　　☐ ⁴ agree
    ☐ ⁵ strongly agree

35. I am sure I can deal with the stresses of adjusting to a culture that is new to me.
    ☐ ¹ strongly disagree　　☐ ² disagree　　☐ ³ neutral　　☐ ⁴ agree
    ☐ ⁵ strongly agree

36. I enjoy living in cultures that are unfamiliar to me.
    ☐ ¹ strongly disagree　　☐ ² disagree　　☐ ³ neutral　　☐ ⁴ agree
    ☐ ⁵ strongly agree

37. I am confident that I can get accustomed to the shopping conditions in a different culture.
    ☐ ¹ strongly disagree　　☐ ² disagree　　☐ ³ neutral　　☐ ⁴ agree
    ☐ ⁵ strongly agree

38. I change my verbal behavior (e.g. accent, tone) when a cross-cultural interaction requires it.
    ☐ ¹ strongly disagree　　☐ ² disagree　　☐ ³ neutral　　☐ ⁴ agree
    ☐ ⁵ strongly agree

39. I use pause and silence differently to suit different cross-cultural situations.
    ☐ ¹ strongly disagree　　☐ ² disagree　　☐ ³ neutral　　☐ ⁴ agree
    ☐ ⁵ strongly agree

40. I vary the rate of my speaking when a cross-cultural situation requires it.
    - ☐ ¹ strongly disagree
    - ☐ ² disagree
    - ☐ ³ neutral
    - ☐ ⁴ agree
    - ☐ ⁵ strongly agree

41. I change my non-verbal behavior when a cross-cultural situation requires it.
    - ☐ ¹ strongly disagree
    - ☐ ² disagree
    - ☐ ³ neutral
    - ☐ ⁴ agree
    - ☐ ⁵ strongly agree

42. I alter my facial expressions when a cross-cultural interaction requires it.
    - ☐ ¹ strongly disagree
    - ☐ ² disagree
    - ☐ ³ neutral
    - ☐ ⁴ agree
    - ☐ ⁵ strongly agree

Appendix B Questionnaire (Chinese)

感谢您参与此次问卷调查。本问卷是在自愿的基础上进行的，仅用于学术目的，收集的信息不涉及您的隐私并将保密。您的回答仅用于数据分析，问卷中的问题仅征询您的看法并无对错之分。您可以跳过任何您觉得不舒服的问题。

第一部分：基本信息

1. 您的性别：
   ☐¹ 男   ☐² 女

2. 您的年龄：
   _____ 岁

3. 您从事出口销售工作年限：
   _____ 年

4. 您的工作地点（城市名）：
   _____

5. 您的受教育水平：
   ☐¹ 高中 / 中专
   ☐² 大专
   ☐³ 本科
   ☐⁴ 研究生及以上

6. 您的月薪：
　　□¹ 5000 元以下（含 5000 元）
　　□² 5001—8000 元
　　□³ 8001—12000 元
　　□⁴ 12001 元以上（含 12001 元）

7. 您的英语水平：
　　□¹ 大学英语四级以下
　　□² 大学英语四级
　　□³ 大学英语六级 / 英语专业四级
　　□⁴ 英语专业八级及以上

8. 您的职位：
　　□¹ 销售代表　　　　□² 销售经理　　　　□³ 销售总监

9. 您的客户类型：
　　□¹ B2B　　　　　　□² B2C　　　　　　□³ B2B 和 B2C

10. 出口国家（请填写您负责销售的产品所销往的目的国家名称，按照销售额数量从高到低进行排列，最多填写三个国家）：
　　_____

11. 您销售的产品所属行业：
　　□¹ 工业用品　　　　□² 消费品

第二部分：关于社交媒体在销售过程中的使用
请选择您在以下七个销售过程中使用的社交媒体种类及使用频率。（若您使用的社交媒体不在以下列表中，欢迎您在表后予以补充。补充时只需说明您使用的社交媒体名称即可。）

Social Media Use in Chinese Export Sales
社交媒体在中国出口销售中的应用

1A. 在您**寻找商业机会**时，您会使用下列哪一种或几种社交媒体？

Facebook	YouTube	WhatsApp	Facebook Messenger	WeChat
Skype	QQ	Q zone	LinkedIn	Instagram
Reddit	Twitter	Vkontakte	TikTok	Sina Weibo
Vimeo	Snapchat	Viber+	Pinterest	LINE
Karao Talk	Google+	Tumblr		

1B. 在您**寻找商业机会**时，您使用以上所选社交媒体的频率是：

☐ ^{1} 从不　　☐ ^{2} 很少　　☐ ^{3} 有时　　☐ ^{4} 常常　　☐ ^{5} 很多时候

2A. 在您**接触顾客之前，进行销售前期调查**时，您会使用下列哪一种或几种社交媒体？

Facebook	YouTube	WhatsApp	Facebook Messenger	WeChat
Skype	QQ	Q zone	LinkedIn	Instagram
Reddit	Twitter	Vkontakte	TikTok	Sina Weibo
Vimeo	Snapchat	Viber+	Pinterest	LINE
Karao Talk	Google+	Tumblr		

APPENDICES 109

2B. 在您**接触顾客之前，进行销售前期调查**时，您使用以上所选社交媒体的频率是：

☐ ¹ 从不　　☐ ² 很少　　☐ ³ 有时　　☐ ⁴ 常常　　☐ ⁵ 很多时候

3A. 在您**与客户进行接洽**时，您使用下列哪一种或几种社交媒体？

Facebook	YouTube	WhatsApp	Facebook Messenger	WeChat
Skype	QQ	Q zone	LinkedIn	Instagram
Reddit	Twitter	Vkontakte	TikTok	Sina Weibo
Vimeo	Snapchat	Viber+	Pinterest	LINE
Karao Talk	Google+	Tumblr		

3B. 在您**与客户进行接洽**时，您使用以上所选社交媒体的频率是：

☐ ¹ 从不　　☐ ² 很少　　☐ ³ 有时　　☐ ⁴ 常常　　☐ ⁵ 很多时候

4A. 在您**介绍产品或展示产品**时，您会使用下列哪一种或几种社交媒体？

Facebook	YouTube	WhatsApp	Facebook Messenger	WeChat
Skype	QQ	Q zone	LinkedIn	Instagram
Reddit	Twitter	Vkontakte	TikTok	Sina Weibo
Vimeo	Snapchat	Viber+	Pinterest	LINE
Karao Talk	Google+	Tumblr		

Social Media Use in Chinese Export Sales
社交媒体在中国出口销售中的应用

4B. 在您**介绍产品或展示产品**时，您使用以上所选社交媒体的频率是：

☐¹ 从不　　☐² 很少　　☐³ 有时　　☐⁴ 常常　　☐⁵ 很多时候

5A. 在您**应对客户不同意见，试图消除客户疑虑**时，您会使用下列哪一种或几种社交媒体？

Facebook	YouTube	WhatsApp	Facebook Messenger	WeChat
Skype	QQ	Q zone	LinkedIn	Instagram
Reddit	Twitter	Vkontakte	TikTok	Sina Weibo
Vimeo	Snapchat	Viber+	Pinterest	LINE
Karao Talk	Google+	Tumblr		

5B. 在您**应对客户不同意见，试图消除客户疑虑**时，您使用以上所选社交媒体的频率是：

☐¹ 从不　　☐² 很少　　☐³ 有时　　☐⁴ 常常　　☐⁵ 很多时候

6A. 在您**达成交易**时，您会使用下列哪一种或几种社交媒体？

Facebook	YouTube	WhatsApp	Facebook Messenger	WeChat
Skype	QQ	Q zone	LinkedIn	Instagram

APPENDICES 111

Reddit	Twitter	Vkontakte	TikTok	Sina Weibo
Vimeo	Snapchat	Viber+	Pinterest	LINE
Karao Talk	Google+	Tumblr		

6B. 在您**达成交易**时，您使用以上所选社交媒体的频率是：

☐ ¹ 从不　　☐ ² 很少　　☐ ³ 有时　　☐ ⁴ 常常　　☐ ⁵ 很多时候

7A. 在您提供**售后跟踪服务**的过程中，您会使用下列哪一种或几种社交媒体？

Facebook	YouTube	WhatsApp	Facebook Messenger	WeChat
Skype	QQ	Q zone	LinkedIn	Instagram
Reddit	Twitter	Vkontakte	TikTok	Sina Weibo
Vimeo	Snapchat	Viber+	Pinterest	LINE
Karao Talk	Google+	Tumblr		

7B. 在您提供**售后跟踪服务**的过程中，您使用以上所选社交媒体的频率是：

☐ ¹ 从不　　☐ ² 很少　　☐ ³ 有时　　☐ ⁴ 常常　　☐ ⁵ 很多时候

第三部分：关于确定客户的能力

请根据以下陈述选择与您能力相符的选项。

8. 我定位客户需求和分析客户需求的能力：
   ☐ [1] 需要提高　　☐ [2] 一般　　☐ [3] 好　　☐ [4] 良好
   ☐ [5] 出色

9. 我了解客户购买动机的能力：
   ☐ [1] 需要提高　　☐ [2] 一般　　☐ [3] 好　　☐ [4] 良好
   ☐ [5] 出色

10. 我识别不同类别客户的能力：
    ☐ [1] 需要提高　　☐ [2] 一般　　☐ [3] 好　　☐ [4] 良好
    ☐ [5] 出色

第四部分：关于适应性销售行为

对于以下陈述，请选择与您实际感受或体会最相符的选项。

11. 当我觉得我的销售策略没有效果时，我能轻松地转换另一种销售方法。
    ☐ [1] 强烈不同意　　☐ [2] 不同意　　☐ [3] 中立　　☐ [4] 同意
    ☐ [5] 强烈同意

12. 我愿意尝试不同的销售策略。
    ☐ [1] 强烈不同意　　☐ [2] 不同意　　☐ [3] 中立　　☐ [4] 同意
    ☐ [5] 强烈同意

13. 我能灵活使用不同的销售策略。
    ☐ [1] 强烈不同意　　☐ [2] 不同意　　☐ [3] 中立　　☐ [4] 同意
    ☐ [5] 强烈同意

14. 我能轻松运用广泛的销售策略。
    ☐ [1] 强烈不同意　　☐ [2] 不同意　　☐ [3] 中立　　☐ [4] 同意
    ☐ [5] 强烈同意

15. 我愿意努力去了解某个客户与其他客户的不同。
    □ ¹ 强烈不同意　　　□ ² 不同意　　　□ ³ 中立　　　□ ⁴ 同意
    □ ⁵ 强烈同意

第五部分：关于销售表现
请评价您在以下几个方面的表现。

16. 在售出高利润产品方面：
    □ ¹ 需要提高　　□ ² 可以接受　　□ ³ 好　　□ ⁴ 良好　　□ ⁵ 优秀

17. 在带来高销售额方面：
    □ ¹ 需要提高　　□ ² 可以接受　　□ ³ 好　　□ ⁴ 良好　　□ ⁵ 优秀

18. 在迅速带来新产品销售业绩方面：
    □ ¹ 需要提高　　□ ² 可以接受　　□ ³ 好　　□ ⁴ 良好　　□ ⁵ 优秀

19. 在超过销售目标方面：
    □ ¹ 需要提高　　□ ² 可以接受　　□ ³ 好　　□ ⁴ 良好　　□ ⁵ 优秀

对于以下陈述，请选择与您实际情况最相符的选项。

20. 同去年相比，我的新客户增加了。
    □ ¹ 强烈不同意　　　□ ² 不同意　　　□ ³ 中立　　　□ ⁴ 同意
    □ ⁵ 强烈同意

21. 同去年相比，我的高质量客户/潜在客户数量增加了。
    □ ¹ 强烈不同意　　　□ ² 不同意　　　□ ³ 中立　　　□ ⁴ 同意
    □ ⁵ 强烈同意

22. 同去年相比，我的客户保持率上涨了。
    □ ¹ 强烈不同意　　　□ ² 不同意　　　□ ³ 中立　　　□ ⁴ 同意
    □ ⁵ 强烈同意

第六部分：关于文化智力

对于以下陈述，请选择与您实际感受或体会最相符的选项。

23. 我有意识在与不同文化背景的人交往时应用文化知识。
    - □ 1 强烈不同意
    - □ 2 不同意
    - □ 3 中立
    - □ 4 同意
    - □ 5 强烈同意

24. 当与来自陌生文化的人们交往时，我能灵活运用自己的文化知识。
    - □ 1 强烈不同意
    - □ 2 不同意
    - □ 3 中立
    - □ 4 同意
    - □ 5 强烈同意

25. 我有意识在跨文化交往时应用文化知识。
    - □ 1 强烈不同意
    - □ 2 不同意
    - □ 3 中立
    - □ 4 同意
    - □ 5 强烈同意

26. 当与来自不同文化的人们交往时，我会审视自己文化知识的准确性。
    - □ 1 强烈不同意
    - □ 2 不同意
    - □ 3 中立
    - □ 4 同意
    - □ 5 强烈同意

27. 我了解其他国家的法律和经济体系。
    - □ 1 强烈不同意
    - □ 2 不同意
    - □ 3 中立
    - □ 4 同意
    - □ 5 强烈同意

28. 我了解其他语言的规则（如词汇、语法）。
    - □ 1 强烈不同意
    - □ 2 不同意
    - □ 3 中立
    - □ 4 同意
    - □ 5 强烈同意

29. 我了解其他文化的价值观和宗教信仰。
    - □ 1 强烈不同意
    - □ 2 不同意
    - □ 3 中立
    - □ 4 同意
    - □ 5 强烈同意

30. 我了解其他文化的婚姻体系。
    - □ 1 强烈不同意
    - □ 2 不同意
    - □ 3 中立
    - □ 4 同意
    - □ 5 强烈同意

31. 我了解其他文化的艺术和工艺品。
    □ ¹ 强烈不同意   □ ² 不同意   □ ³ 中立   □ ⁴ 同意
    □ ⁵ 强烈同意

32. 我了解其他文化中表达非语言行为的规则。
    □ ¹ 强烈不同意   □ ² 不同意   □ ³ 中立   □ ⁴ 同意
    □ ⁵ 强烈同意

33. 我喜欢与来自不同文化的人交往。
    □ ¹ 强烈不同意   □ ² 不同意   □ ³ 中立   □ ⁴ 同意
    □ ⁵ 强烈同意

34. 我相信自己能够在陌生文化中与当地人进行交往。
    □ ¹ 强烈不同意   □ ² 不同意   □ ³ 中立   □ ⁴ 同意
    □ ⁵ 强烈同意

35. 我相信自己可以应对因适应新文化而造成的额外压力。
    □ ¹ 强烈不同意   □ ² 不同意   □ ³ 中立   □ ⁴ 同意
    □ ⁵ 强烈同意

36. 我喜欢生活在自己不熟悉的文化中。
    □ ¹ 强烈不同意   □ ² 不同意   □ ³ 中立   □ ⁴ 同意
    □ ⁵ 强烈同意

37. 我相信自己可以适应不同文化中的购物环境。
    □ ¹ 强烈不同意   □ ² 不同意   □ ³ 中立   □ ⁴ 同意
    □ ⁵ 强烈同意

38. 我根据跨文化交往的需要而改变自己的语言方式（如口音、语调）。
    □ ¹ 强烈不同意   □ ² 不同意   □ ³ 中立   □ ⁴ 同意
    □ ⁵ 强烈同意

39. 我有选择地使用停顿和沉默以适应不同的跨文化交往情境。
    □ ¹ 强烈不同意　　□ ² 不同意　　□ ³ 中立　　□ ⁴ 同意
    □ ⁵ 强烈同意

40. 我能根据跨文化交往的情境需要改变自己的语速。
    □ ¹ 强烈不同意　　□ ² 不同意　　□ ³ 中立　　□ ⁴ 同意
    □ ⁵ 强烈同意

41. 我能根据跨文化交往的情境需要改变自己的非语言行为（如手势、头部动作、站位的远近）。
    □ ¹ 强烈不同意　　□ ² 不同意　　□ ³ 中立　　□ ⁴ 同意
    □ ⁵ 强烈同意

42. 我能根据跨文化交往的情境需要改变自己的面部表情。
    □ ¹ 强烈不同意　　□ ² 不同意　　□ ³ 中立　　□ ⁴ 同意
    □ ⁵ 强烈同意

BIBLIOGRAPHY

Aaker, J. L., & Lee, A. Y. (2001). "I" seek pleasures and "we" avoid pains: The role of self-regulatory goals in information processing and persuasion. *Journal of Consumer Research,* 28(1), 33–49.

Abeza, G., O'Reilly, N., & Reid, I. (2013). Relationship marketing and social media in sport. *International Journal of Sport Communication,* 6(2), 120–142.

Abu ELSamen, A., & Akroush, M. N. (2018). How customer orientation enhances salespeople's performance? A case study from an international market. *Benchmarking: An International Journal,* 25(7), 2460–2477.

Acharya, A. S., Prakash, A., Saxena, P., & Nigam, A. (2013). Sampling: Why and how of it. *Indian Journal of Medical Specialties,* 4(2), 330–333.

Adair, W. L., Hideg, I., & Spence, J. R. (2013). The culturally intelligent team: The impact of team cultural intelligence and cultural heterogeneity on team shared values. *Journal of Cross-Cultural Psychology,* 44(6), 941–962.

Agnihotri, R., Dingus, R., Hu, M. Y., & Krush, M. T. (2016). Social media: Influencing customer satisfaction in B2B sales. *Industrial Marketing Management,* 53, 172–180.

Agnihotri, R., Gabler, C. B., Itani, O. S., Jaramillo, F., & Krush, M. T. (2017). Salesperson ambidexterity and customer satisfaction: Examining the role of customer demandingness, adaptive selling, and role conflict. *Journal of Personal Selling & Sales Management,* 37(1), 27–41.

Agnihotri, R., Kothandaraman, P., Kashyap, R., & Singh, R. (2012). Bringing "social" into sales: The impact of salespeople's social media use on service behaviors and value creation. *Journal of Personal Selling & Sales Management,* 32(3), 333–348.

Ahearne, M., Hughes, D. E., & Schillewaert, N. (2007). Why sales reps should welcome information technology: Measuring the impact of CRM-based IT on sales effectiveness. *International Journal of Research in Marketing,* 24(4), 336–349.

Ahearne, M., Jelinek, R., & Rapp, A. (2005). Moving beyond the direct effect of SFA adoption on salesperson performance: training and support as key moderating factors. *Industrial Marketing Management,* 34(4), 379–388.

Ahearne, M., Jones, E., Rapp, A., & Mathieu, J. (2008). High touch through high tech: The impact of salesperson technology usage on sales performance via mediating mechanisms. *Management Science,* 54(4), 671–685.

Elyasi, F., Ahmadi, M., Moalemkoale, N.M., Jafari, S. N. Hoseini, S. M., & Hoseini, S. H. (2017). Relationship between Cultural Intelligence and Mental Health in Students of the Medical University of Mazandaran in 2017. *Future of Medical Education Journal,* 7(3), 34–39.

Ainin, S., Parveen, F., Moghavvemi, S., Jaafar, N. I., & Mohd Shuib, N. L. (2015). Factors influencing the use of social media by SMEs and its performance outcomes. *Industrial Management & Data Systems,* 115(3), 570–588.

Alalwan, A. A., Rana, N. P., Dwivedi, Y. K., & Algharabat, R. (2017). Social media in marketing: A review and analysis of the existing literature. *Telematics and Informatics,* 34(7), 1177–1190.

Alarcón-del-Amo, M. d. C., Rialp-Criado, A., & Rialp-Criado, J. (2018). Examining the impact of managerial involvement with social media on exporting firm performance. *International Business Review,* 27(2), 355-366.

Alarcón-del-Amo, M. d. C., Rialp-Criado, A., & Rialp-Criado, J. (2016). Social media adoption by exporters: The export-dependence moderating role. *Spanish Journal of Marketing – ESIC,* 20(2), 81-92. doi:10.1016/j.sjme.2016.07.002

Alarcón-del-Amo, M. d. C., Rialp-Criado, A., & Rialp-Criado, J. (2015). The effect of social media adoption on exporting firms' performance. In *Entrepreneurship in international marketing* (Vol. 25, pp. 161-186). Emerald Group Publishing Limited.

Alba, J. W., & Hutchinson, J. W. (1987). Dimensions of consumer expertise. *Journal of Consumer Research,* 13(4), 411-454.

Anderson, E., & Oliver, R. L. (1987). Perspectives on behavior-based versus outcome-based salesforce control systems. *The Journal of marketing,* 51(4), 76-88.

Anderson, R. E., Dixon, A. L., Jones, E., Johnston, M. W., LaForge, R. W., Marshall, G. W., & Tanner Jr., J. F. (2005). The scholarship of teaching in sales education. *Marketing Education Review,* 15(2), 1-10.

Andzulis, J. M., Panagopoulos, N. G., & Rapp, A. (2012). A review of social media and implications for the sales process. *Journal of Personal Selling & Sales Management,* 32(3), 305-316.

Ang, S., & Inkpen, A. C. (2008). Cultural intelligence and offshore outsourcing success: A framework of firm-level intercultural capability. *Decision Sciences,* 39(3), 337-358.

Ang, S., & Van Dyne, L. (2008). *Handbook of Cultural Intelligence: Theory, Measurement, and Applications.* New York: M.E. Sharpe, Inc.

Ang, S., & Van Dyne, L. (2015). *Handbook of cultural intelligence.* Routledge.

Ang, S., Van Dyne, L., Koh, C., Ng, K. Y., Templer, K. J., Tay, C., & Chandrasekar, N. A. (2007). Cultural intelligence: Its measurement and effects on cultural judgment and decision making, cultural adaptation and task performance. *Management and organization review,* 3(3), 335–371.

Van Dyne L., Ang, S., & Tan, M. L. (2008). *Cultural intelligence. The Cambridge.*

Arli, D., Bauer, C., & Palmatier, R. W. (2018). Relational selling: Past, present and future. *Industrial Marketing Management,* 69, 169–184.

Armstrong, J. S., & Overton, T. S. (1977). Estimating nonresponse bias in mail surveys. *Journal of marketing Research,* 14(3), 396–402.

Arnaboldi, M., & Coget, J.-F. (2016). Social media and business: We've been asking the wrong question. *Organizational Dynamics,* 45(1), 47–54.

Babakus, E., Cravens, D. W., Grant, K., Ingram, T. N., & LaForge, R. W. (1996). Investigating the relationships among sales, management control, sales territory design, salesperson performance, and sales organization effectiveness. *International Journal of Research in Marketing,* 13(4), 345–363.

Babakus, E., Cravens, D. W., Johnston, M., & Moncrief, W. C. (1999). The role of emotional exhaustion in sales force attitude and behavior relationships. *Journal of the Academy of Marketing Science,* 27(1), 58–70.

Bakker, A. B., & Demerouti, E. (2007). The job demands–resources model: State of the art. *Journal of managerial psychology,* 22(3), 309–328.

Baldauf, A., & Cravens, D. W. (2002). The effect of moderators on the salesperson behavior performance and salesperson outcome performance and sales organization effectiveness relationships. *European Journal of Marketing,* 36(11/12), 1367–1388.

Ball, D., Coelho, P. S., & Machás, A. (2004). The role of communication and trust in explaining customer loyalty: An extension to the ECSI model. *European Journal of Marketing,* 38(9/10), 1272–1293.

Baltaci, A. (2017). Relations between prejudice, cultural intelligence and level of entrepreneurship: A study of school principals. *International Electronic Journal of Elementary Education,* 9(3), 645–666.

Banin, A. Y., Boso, N., Hultman, M., Souchon, A. L., Hughes, P., & Nemkova, E. (2016). Salesperson improvisation: Antecedents, performance outcomes, and boundary conditions. *Industrial Marketing Management,* 59, 120–130.

Barakat, L. L., Lorenz, M. P., Ramsey, J. R., & Cretoiu, S. L. (2015). Global managers: An analysis of the impact of cultural intelligence on job satisfaction and performance. *International Journal of Emerging Markets,* 10(4), 781–800.

Barker, A. T. (1999). Benchmarks of successful salesforce performance. *Canadian Journal of Administrative Sciences/Revue Canadienne des Sciences de l' Administration,* 16(2), 95–104.

Barker, K., Day, C. R., Day, D. L., Kujava, E. R., Otwori, J., Ruscitto, R. A., Smith, A. Xu, T. (2017). Global communication and cross-cultural competence: Twenty-first century micro-case studies. *Global Advances in Business Communication,* 6(1), 5.

Barnes, D., Clear, F., Dyerson, R., Harindranath, G., Harris, L., & Rae, A. (2012). Web 2.0 and micro-businesses: An exploratory investigation. *Journal of Small Business and Enterprise Development,* 19(4), 687–711.

Barney, J. (1991). Firm resources and sustained competitive advantage. *Journal of management,* 17(1), 99–120.

Bartkus, K. R., Peterson, M. F., & Bellenger, D. N. (1989). Type a behavior, experience, and salesperson performance. *Journal of Personal Selling & Sales Management,* 9(2), 11–18.

Bauman, A. A., & Shcherbina, N. V. (2018). Millennials, technology, and cross-cultural communication. *Journal of Higher Education Theory & Practice,* 18(3), 75–85.

Beese, J. (2011).Social networks influence 74% of consumers' buying decisions. *Sproutsocial, November* 16th.

Behrman, D. N., & Perreault Jr., W. D. (1982). Measuring the performance of industrial salespersons. *Journal of Business Research,* 10(3), 355–370.

Bell, E., Bryman, A., & Harley, B. (2018). *Business research methods*. Oxford University Press.

Bocconcelli, R., Cioppi, M., & Pagano, A. (2017). Social media as a resource in SMEs' sales process. *Journal of Business & Industrial Marketing,* 32(5), 693–709.

Boorom, M. L., Goolsby, J. R., & Ramsey, R. P. (1998). Relational communication traits and their effect on adaptiveness and sales performance. *Journal of the Academy of Marketing Science,* 26(1), 16–30.

Borman, W. C., Hanson, M. A., Oppler, S. H., Pulakos, E. D., & White, L. A. (1993). Role of early supervisory experience in supervisor performance. *Journal of Applied Psychology,* 78(3), 443.

Brennan, R., & Croft, R. (2012). The use of social media in B2B marketing and branding: An exploratory study. *Journal of Customer Behaviour,* 11(2), 101–115.

Brislin, R., Worthley, R., & Macnab, B. (2006). Cultural intelligence: Understanding behaviors that serve people's goals. *Group & Organization Management,* 31(1), 40–55.

Brislin, R. (1970). Back-translation for cross-cultural research. *Journal of Cross-Cultural Psychology,* 1(3), 185–216.

Brown, S. P., & Peterson, R. A. (1993). Antecedents and consequences of salesperson job satisfaction: Meta-analysis and assessment of causal effects. *Journal of Marketing Research,* 30(1), 63–77.

Bruner, J. S. (1957). On perceptual readiness. *Psychological Review,* 64(2), 123.

Bruner, J. S., Goodnow, J. J., & Austin, G. A.(1956). *A study of thinking*. John Wiley & Sons.

Bstieler, L., & Hemmert, M. (2008). Developing trust in vertical product development partnerships: A comparison of South Korea and Austria. *Journal of World Business,* 43(1), 35–46.

Bücker, J. J. L. E., Furrer, O., Poutsma, E., & Buyens, D. (2014). The impact of cultural intelligence on communication effectiveness, job satisfaction and anxiety for Chinese host country managers working for foreign multinationals. *The International Journal of Human Resource Management,* 25(14), 2068–2087.

Cantor, N., & Mischel, W. (1979). Prototypes in person perception. In *Advances in Experimental Social Psychology* (Vol. 12, pp. 3–52). Elsevier.

Castañeda, D. R., Huang, A., & Avalos, A. R. (2018). Willingness to learn: Cultural intelligence effect on perspective taking and multicultural creativity. *International Business Research,* 11(2), 116–124.

Chakrabarty, S., Brown, G., Widing, R. E., & Taylor, R. D. (2004). Analysis and recommendations for the alternative measures of adaptive selling. *Journal of Personal Selling & Sales Management,* 24(2), 125–133.

Chakrabarty, S., Widing, R. E., & Brown, G. (2014). Selling behaviours and sales performance: The moderating and mediating effects of interpersonal mentalizing. *Journal of Personal Selling & Sales Management,* 34(2), 112–122.

Challagalla, G. N., & Shervani, T. A. (1996). Dimensions and types of supervisory control: Effects on salesperson performance and satisfaction. *Journal of Marketing,* 60(1), 89–105.

Chang, W., Park, J. E., & Chaiy, S. (2010). How does CRM technology transform into organizational performance? A mediating role of marketing capability. *Journal of Business Research,* 63(8), 849–855.

Charoensukmongkol, P. (2014). Effects of support and job demands on social media use and work outcomes. *Computers in Human Behavior,* 36, 340–349.

Charoensukmongkol, P. (2015a). Cultural intelligence of entrepreneurs and international network ties: The case of small and medium manufacturing firms in Thailand. *Management Research Review,* 38(4), 421–436.

Charoensukmongkol, P. (2015b). Social media use and job performance: Moderating roles of workplace factors. *International Journal of Cyber Behavior, Psychology and Learning,* 5(2), 59–74. doi:10.4018/IJCBPL.2015040105

Charoensukmongkol, P. (2016a). Cultural intelligence and export performance of small and medium enterprises in Thailand: Mediating roles of organizational capabilities. *International Small Business Journal,* 34(1), 105–122.

Charoensukmongkol, P. (2016b). Exploring personal characteristics associated with selfie-liking. *Cyberpsychology: Journal of Psychosocial Research on Cyberspace,* 10(2), article 7.

Charoensukmongkol, P. (2016c). The interconnections between bribery, political network, government supports, and their consequences on export performance of small and medium enterprises in Thailand. *Journal of International Entrepreneurship,* 14(2), 259–276.

Charoensukmongkol, P. (2016d). The role of mindfulness on employee psychological reactions to mergers and acquisitions. *Journal of Organizational Change Management,* 29(5), 816–831.

Charoensukmongkol, P. (2017). Contributions of mindfulness during post-merger integration. *Journal of Managerial Psychology,* 32(1), 104–118.

Charoensukmongkol, P. (2019a). Contributions of mindfulness to improvisational behavior and consequences on business performance and stress of entrepreneurs during economic downturn. *Organization Management Journal,* 16(4), 209–219.

Charoensukmongkol, P. (2019b). The efficacy of cultural intelligence for adaptive selling behaviors in cross-cultural selling: The moderating effect of trait mindfulness. *Journal of Global Marketing,* 33(3), 141–157.

Charoensukmongkol, P. (2019c). The moderating effect of locus of control on the relationship between perceived poor business performance and superstitious behaviors of Thai entrepreneurs. *BU Academic Review,* 18(1), 1–17.

Charoensukmongkol, P. (2019d). The role of mindfulness in reducing English language anxiety among Thai college students. *International Journal of Bilingual Education and Bilingualism,* 22(4), 414–427.

Charoensukmongkol, P., & Aumeboonsuke, V. (2017). Does mindfulness enhance stock trading performance? The moderating and mediating effects of impulse control difficulties. *International Journal of Work Organisation and Emotion,* 7(4), 257–274.

Charoensukmongkol, P., Daniel, J. L., & Chatelain-Jardon, R. (2013). Enhancing workplace spirituality through emotional intelligence. *Journal of Applied Management and Entrepreneurship,* 18(4), 3-17.

Charoensukmongkol, P., Daniel, J. L., & Chatelain-Jardon, R. (2015). The contribution of workplace spirituality on organizational citizenship behavior. *Advances in Business Research,* 6(1), 32-45.

Charoensukmongkol, P., Murad, M., & Gutierrez-Wirsching, S. (2016). The Role of coworker and supervisor support on Job burnout and job satisfaction. *Journal of Advances in Management Research,* 13(1), 4-22.

Charoensukmongkol, P., & Sasatanun, P. (2017). Social media use for CRM and business performance satisfaction: The moderating roles of social skills and social media sales intensity. *Asia Pacific Management Review,* 22(1), 25-34.

Charoensukmongkol, P., & Suthatorn, P. (2018). Salespeople's trait mindfulness and emotional exhaustion: The mediating roles of optimism, resilience, and self-efficacy. *International Journal of Services, Economics and Management,* 9(2), 125-142.

Chen, A. S., Wu, I., & Bian, M. (2014). The moderating effects of active and agreeable conflict management styles on cultural intelligence and cross-cultural adjustment. *International Journal of Cross Cultural Management,* 14(3), 270-288.

Chen, C. C., & Jaramillo, F. (2014). The double-edged effects of emotional intelligence on the adaptive selling–salesperson-owned loyalty relationship. *Journal of Personal Selling & Sales Management,* 34(1), 33-50.

Chen, G., Kirkman, B. L., Kim, K., Farh, C. I., & Tangirala, S. (2010). When does cross-cultural motivation enhance expatriate effectiveness? A multilevel investigation of the moderating roles of subsidiary support and cultural distance. *Academy of Management Journal,* 53(5), 1110-1130.

Chen, R. R., Ou, C. X., Wang, W., Peng, Z., & Davison, R. M. (2015). Moving beyond the direct impact of using CRM systems on frontline employees' service performance: The mediating role of adaptive behaviour. *Information Systems Journal,* 30(3), 458–491.

Chen, X. P., Liu, D., & Portnoy, R. (2012). A multilevel investigation of motivational cultural intelligence, organizational diversity climate, and cultural sales: Evidence from US real estate firms. *Journal of Applied Psychology,* 97(1), 93.

Chen, Y. C., Rivas, A. A., & Wu, W. Y. (2018). Exploring the determinants and consequences of salesperson market orientation behavior: An empirical study in the financial service industry. *Journal of Service Theory and Practice,* 28(2), 170–195.

Chesbrough, H. (2011). Bringing open innovation to services. *MIT Sloan Management Review,* 52(2), 85–90.

Chin, W. W. (1998). The partial least squares approach to structural equation modeling. *Modern Methods for Business Research,* 295(2), 295–336.

Chin, W. W. (2010). How to write up and report PLS analyses. In *Handbook of Partial Least Squares* (pp. 655–690). Berlin: Springer.

Chin, W. W., Marcolin, B. L., & Newsted, P. R. (2003). A partial least squares latent variable modeling approach for measuring interaction effects: Results from a Monte Carlo simulation study and an electronic-mail emotion/adoption study. *Information Systems Research,* 14(2), 189–217.

Choudhury, M. M., & Harrigan, P. (2014). CRM to social CRM: The integration of new technologies into customer relationship management. *Journal of Strategic Marketing,* 22(2), 149–176.

Chu, S. C., & Kim, Y. (2011). Determinants of consumer engagement in electronic word-of-mouth (eWOM) in social networking sites. *International Journal of Advertising,* 30(1), 47–75.

Chua, R. Y., Morris, M. W., & Mor, S. (2012). Collaborating across cultures: Cultural metacognition and affect-based trust in creative collaboration. *Organizational Behavior and Human Decision Processes,* 118(2), 116–131.

Churchill Jr., G. A., Ford, N. M., Hartley, S. W., & Walker Jr., O. C. (1985). The determinants of salesperson performance: A meta-analysis. *Journal of Marketing Research,* 22(2), 103–118.

Clark, L. A., & Watson, D. (1995). Constructing validity: Basic issues in objective scale development. *Psychological Assessment,* 7(3), 3093–9.

Clarke, W. M. (1999). An assessment of foreign language training for English-speaking exporters. *Journal of European Industrial Training,* 23(1), 9–15.

Cohen, C. E. (1977). Cognitive basis of stereotyping. Paper presented at the *meeting of the American Psychological Association,* San Francisco.

Cohen, J., & Basu, K. (1987). Alternative models of categorization: toward a contingent processing framework. *Journal of Consumer Research,* 13(4), 455–472.

Conway, J. M., & Lance, C. E. (2010). What reviewers should expect from authors regarding common method bias in organizational research. *Journal of Business and Psychology,* 25(3), 325–334.

Cotham, J. C. (1969). Using personal history information in retail salesman selection. *Journal of Retailing,* 45(2), 31.

Cox, J. L., Martinez, E. R., & Quinlan, K. B. (2008). Blogs and the corporation: Managing the risk, reaping the benefits. *Journal of Business Strategy,* 29(3), 4–12.

Cravens, D. W., Ingram, T. N., LaForge, R. W., & Young, C. E. (1993). Behavior-based and outcome-based salesforce control systems. *The Journal of Marketing*, 47–59.

Crick, D. (1999). An investigation into SMEs' use of languages in their export operations. *International Journal of Entrepreneurial Behavior & Research,* 5(1), 19–31.

Crowne, K. A. (2008). What leads to cultural intelligence? *Business horizons,* 51(5), 391–399.

Customs, C. (2019). *China Import and Export Value in* 2018. China Customs. http://www.customs.gov.cn/customs/302249/302274/302275/2166524/index.html

De Vaus, D. (2013). *Surveys in social research*: Routledge.

De Vries, L., Gensler, S., & Leeflang, P. S. H. (2012). Popularity of brand posts on brand fan pages: An investigation of the effects of social media marketing. *Journal of Interactive Marketing,* 26(2), 83–91.

Dehghani, M., & Tumer, M. (2015). A research on effectiveness of Facebook advertising on enhancing purchase intention of consumers. *Computers in Human Behavior,* 49, 597–600.

DelVecchio, S. K. (1998). The quality of salesperson–manager relationship: The effect of latitude, loyalty and competence. *Journal of Personal Selling & Sales Management,* 18(1), 31–47.

Dolan, R., Conduit, J., Fahy, J., & Goodman, S. (2017). Social media: communication strategies, engagement and future research directions. *International Journal of Wine Business Research,* 29(1), 2–19.

Dong, J. Q., & Wu, W. (2015). Business value of social media technologies: Evidence from online user innovation communities. *The Journal of Strategic Information Systems,* 24(2), 113–127.

Draper, N. R., & Smith, H. (1998). *Applied regression analysis* (Vol. 326). John Wiley & Sons.

Duffett, R. G. (2015). Facebook advertising's influence on intention-to-purchase and purchase amongst Millennials. *Internet Research,* 25(4), 498–526.

Durkin, M., McGowan, P., & McKeown, N. (2013). Exploring social media adoption in small to medium-sized enterprises in Ireland. *Journal of Small Business and Enterprise Development,* 20(4), 716–734.

Eagleman, A. N. (2013). Acceptance, motivations, and usage of social media as a marketing communications tool amongst employees of sport national governing bodies. *Sport Management Review,* 16(4), 488–497.

Earley, P. C., & Ang, S. (2003). *Cultural intelligence: Individual interactions across cultures.* Stanford University Press.

Eccles, J. S., & Wigfield, A. (2002). Motivational beliefs, values, and goals. *Annual Review of Psychology,* 53(1), 109–132.

Efron, B. (1982). *The jackknife, the bootstrap, and other resampling plans* (Vol. 38). Philadelphia: Society for Industrial and Applied Mathematics.

Enderwick, P., & Akoorie, M. (1994). Pilot study research note: The employment of foreign language specialists and export success–The case of New Zealand. *International Marketing Review,* 11(4), 4–18.

Enderwick, P., & Gray, D. (1993). Foreign languages in international business: The case of New Zealand. *Journal of Teaching in International Business,* 4(1), 49–68.

Erkan, I., & Evans, C. (2016). The influence of eWOM in social media on consumers' purchase intentions: An extended approach to information adoption. *Computers in Human Behavior*, 61, 47–55.

Facebook. (2016). *Facebook Annual report* 2016. http://www.annualreports.com/HostedData/AnnualReportArchive/f/NASDAQ_FB_2016.pdf

Falls, J. (2009). Public relations pros must be social media ready. *Social Media Explorer*, 10, 2009.

Fang, E., Palmatier, R. W., & Evans, K. R. (2004). Goal-setting paradoxes? Trade-offs between working hard and working smart: The United States versus China. *Journal of the Academy of Marketing Science*, 32(2), 188–202.

Farrar, D. E., & Glauber, R. R. (1967). Multicollinearity in regression analysis: The problem revisited. *The Review of Economic and Statistics*, 92–107.

Farrell, W. C., & Hutasingh, T. (2018). Cross cultural communication between developed and emerging markets: A qualitative study on small and medium-sized enterprise communication technology selection and utilisation. *International Journal of Globalisation and Small Business*, 10(1), 1–20.

Featherstonehaugh, B. (2010). *The future of selling: It's social*. www.Forbes.com.

Ford, N. M., Walker Jr., O. C., Churchill Jr., G. A., & Hartley, S. W. (1987). Selecting successful salespeople: A meta-analysis of biographical and psychological selection criteria. *Review of marketing*, 10, 90–131.

Fornell, C., & Larcker, D. F. (1981). Evaluating structural equation models with unobservable variables and measurement error. *Journal of Marketing Research*, 18(1), 39–50.

Franke, G. R., & Park, J. E. (2006). Salesperson adaptive selling behavior and customer orientation: A meta-analysis. *Journal of Marketing Research,* 43(4), 693–702.

Fred Miao, C., & Evans, K. R. (2007). The impact of salesperson motivation on role perceptions and job performance: A cognitive and affective perspective. *Journal of Personal Selling & Sales Management,* 27(1), 89–101.

Freedman, D. A. (2009). *Statistical models: theory and practice.* Cambridge University Press.

Gamboa, A. M., & Goncalves, H. M. (2014). Customer loyalty through social networks: Lessons from Zara on Facebook. *Business Horizons,* 57(6), 709–717.

Gao, Q., & Feng, C. (2016). Branding with social media: User gratifications, usage patterns, and brand message content strategies. *Computers in Human Behavior,* 63, 868–890.

Gary, H. (1990). *Practical Sampling.* London: Sage Publications.

Geiger, S., & Turley, D. (2006). The perceived impact of information technology on salespeople's relational competencies. *Journal of Marketing Management,* 22(7–8), 827–851.

Giacobbe, R. W., Jackson Jr., D. W., Crosby, L. A., & Bridges, C. M. (2006). A contingency approach to adaptive selling behavior and sales performance: Selling situations and salesperson characteristics. *Journal of Personal Selling & Sales Management,* 26(2), 115–142.

Gibbs, J. L., Rozaidi, N. A., & Eisenberg, J. (2013). Overcoming the "ideology of openness": Probing the affordances of social media for organizational knowledge sharing. *Journal of Computer-Mediated Communication,* 19(1), 102–120.

Groves, K. S., Feyerherm, A., & Gu, M. (2015). Examining cultural intelligence and cross-cultural negotiation effectiveness. *Journal of Management Education,* 39(2), 209-243.

Groza, M., Peterson, R., Sullivan, U. Y., & Krishnan, V. (2012). Social media and the sales force: The importance of intra-organizational cooperation and training on performance. *The Marketing Management Journal,* 22(2), 118-130.

Guenzi, P., De Luca, L. M., & Spiro, R. (2016). The combined effect of customer perceptions about a salesperson's adaptive selling and selling orientation on customer trust in the salesperson: A contingency perspective. *Journal of Business & Industrial Marketing,* 31(4), 553-564.

Guesalaga, R. (2016). The use of social media in sales: Individual and organizational antecedents, and the role of customer engagement in social media. *Industrial Marketing Management,* 54, 71-79.

Hair, J. F., Black, W. C., Babin, B. J., Anderson, R. E., & Tatham, R. L. (2006). *Multivariate data analysis.* Upper Saddle River, NJ: Pearson Prentice Hall.

Hair, J. F., Ringle, C. M., & Sarstedt, M. (2011). PLS-SEM: Indeed a silver bullet. *Journal of Marketing Theory and Practice,* 19(2), 139-152.

Hair, J. F., Sarstedt, M., Ringle, C. M., & Mena, J. A. (2012). An assessment of the use of partial least squares structural equation modeling in marketing research. *Journal of the Academy of Marketing Science,* 40(3), 414-433.

Hair J. F., Sarstedt, M., Hopkins, L., & G. Kuppelwieser, V. (2014). Partial least squares structural equation modeling (PLS-SEM) An emerging tool in business research. *European Business Review,* 26(2), 106-121.

Hamilton, M., Kaltcheva, V. D., & Rohm, A. J. (2016). Social media and value creation:

The role of interaction satisfaction and interaction immersion. *Journal of Interactive Marketing,* 36(1), 121–133.

Hansen, J. D., Singh, T., Weilbaker, D. C., & Guesalaga, R. (2011). Cultural intelligence in cross-cultural selling: Propositions and directions for future research. *Journal of Personal Selling & Sales Management,* 31(3), 243–254.

Harrigan, P., Evers, U., Miles, M., & Daly, T. (2017). Customer engagement with tourism social media brands. *Tourism Management,* 59, 597–609.

Harrigan, P., Soutar, G., Choudhury, M. M., & Lowe, M. (2015). Modelling CRM in a social media age. *Australasian Marketing Journal,* 23(1), 27–37.

Hedges, L. G. (1972). A study in meaning criteria and the logic of fuzzy concepts. In *8th Regional Meeting of the Chicago Linguistic Society,* pp. 183–228.

Henseler, J., Ringle, C. M., & Sinkovics, R. R. (2009). The use of partial least squares path modeling in international marketing. In *New challenges to international marketing,* pp. 277–319. Emerald Group Publishing Limited.

Hofstede, G. (2001). *Culture's consequences: Comparing values, behaviors, institutions and organizations across nations.* Sage publications.

Hootsuite. (2019). The Best Way to Manage Social Media. https://signupnow.hootsuite.com/apac-management/?utm_source=google&utm_medium=cpc&utm_campaign=selfserve-bau-apac-en-asia-th1-pua-search_nonbranded_alpha&utm_term=social%20media%20marketing&gclid=EAIaIQobChMIpK-ryeeQ5QIVgo2PCh1eiQVnEAAYASAAEgK0FPD_BwE

Hsieh, G., & Kocielnik, R. (2016). You get who you pay for: The impact of incentives on participation bias. *Proceedings of the 19th ACM Conference on Computer-Supported Cooperative Work & Social Computing,* pp. 823–835.

Hu, N., Wu, J., & Gu, J. (2017). Cultural intelligence and employees' creative performance: The moderating role of team conflict in interorganizational teams. *Journal of Management & Organization*, 25(1), 96–116.

Hudson, S., & Hudson, R. (2013). Engaging with consumers using social media: A case study of music festivals. *International Journal of Event and Festival Management*, 4(3), 206–223.

Huff, K. C., Song, P., & Gresch, E. B. (2014). Cultural intelligence, personality, and cross-cultural adjustment: A study of expatriates in Japan. *International Journal of Intercultural Relations*, 38, 151–157.

Hult, G. T. M., Ketchen Jr., D. J., Griffith, D. A., Finnegan, C. A., Gonzalez-Padron, T., Harmancioglu, N., ... Cavusgil, S. T. (2008). Data equivalence in cross-cultural international business research: assessment and guidelines. *Journal of International Business Studies*, 39(6), 1027–1044.

Hunter, G. K., & Perreault Jr., W. D. (2007). Making sales technology effective. *Journal of Marketing*, 71(1), 16–34.

Hyman, L., Lamb, J., & Bulmer, M. (2006). The use of pre-existing survey questions: Implications for data quality. In *Proceedings of the European Conference on Quality in Survey Statistics*, pp. 1–8.

Imai, L., & Gelfand, M. J. (2010). The culturally intelligent negotiator: The impact of cultural intelligence (CQ) on negotiation sequences and outcomes. *Organizational Behavior and Human Decision Processes*, 112(2), 83–98.

Itani, O. S., Agnihotri, R., & Dingus, R. (2017). Social media use in B2B sales and its impact on competitive intelligence collection and adaptive selling: Examining the role of learning orientation as an enabler. *Industrial Marketing Management*, 66, 64–79.

Jaramillo, F., & Grisaffe, D. B. (2009). Does customer orientation impact objective sales performance? Insights from a longitudinal model in direct selling. *Journal of Personal Selling & Sales Management,* 29(2), 167–178.

Jaramillo, F., Locander, W. B., Spector, P. E., & Harris, E. G. (2007). Getting the job done: The moderating role of initiative on the relationship between intrinsic motivation and adaptive selling. *Journal of Personal Selling & Sales Management,* 27(1), 59–74.

Järvinen, J., & Taiminen, H. (2016). Harnessing marketing automation for B2B content marketing. *Industrial Marketing Management,* 54, 164–175.

Johlke, M. C. (2006). Sales presentation skills and salesperson job performance. *Journal of Business & Industrial Marketing,* 21(5), 311–319.

Jones, E., Brown, S. P., Zoltners, A. A., & Weitz, B. A. (2005). The changing environment of selling and sales management. *Journal of Personal Selling & Sales Management,* 25(2), 105–111.

Jones, E., Chonko, L., Rangarajan, D., & Roberts, J. (2007). The role of overload on job attitudes, turnover intentions, and salesperson performance. *Journal of Business Research,* 60(7), 663–671.

Jussila, J. J., Kärkkäinen, H., & Aramo-Immonen, H. (2014). Social media utilization in business-to-business relationships of technology industry firms. *Computers in Human Behavior,* 30, 606–613.

Kadic-Maglajlic, S., Vida, I., Obadia, C., & Plank, R. (2016). Clarifying the influence of emotional intelligence on salesperson performance. *Journal of Business & Industrial Marketing,* 31(7), 877–888.

Kanuk, L., & Berenson, C. (1975). Mail surveys and response rates: A literature review.

Journal of marketing Research, 12(4), 440-453.

Kaplan, A. M., & Haenlein, M. (2010). Users of the world, unite! The challenges and opportunities of Social Media. *Business horizons,* 53(1), 59-68.

Kaptein, M., McFarland, R., & Parvinen, P. (2018). Automated adaptive selling. *European Journal of Marketing,* 52(5/6), 1037-1059.

Karimi, S., & Naghibi, H. S. (2015). Social media marketing (SMM) strategies for small to medium enterprises (SMEs). *International Journal of Information, Business and Management,* 7(4), 86.

Kaski, T., Niemi, J., & Pullins, E. (2018). Rapport building in authentic B2B sales interaction. *Industrial Marketing Management,* 69, 235-252.

Kaynak, E., Kara, A., Chow, C. S., & Laukkanen, T. (2016). Role of adaptive selling and customer orientation on salesperson performance: Evidence from two distinct markets of Europe and Asia. *Journal of Transnational Management,* 21(2), 62-83.

Keenan Jr., W. (1989). The nagging problem of the plateaued salesperson. *Sales and Marketing Management,* 141(4), 36.

Keillor, B. D., Parker, R. S., & Pettijohn, C. E. (2000). Relationship-oriented characteristics and individual salesperson performance. *Journal of Business & Industrial Marketing,* 15(1), 7-22.

Kietzmann, J. H., Hermkens, K., McCarthy, I. P., & Silvestre, B. S. (2011). Social media? Get serious! Understanding the functional building blocks of social media. *Business Horizons,* 54(3), 241-251.

Kietzmann, T. C., Geuter, S., & König, P. (2011). Overt visual attention as a causal factor of perceptual awareness. *PloS one,* 6(7), e22614.

Klein, D. F. (2005). Beyond significance testing: Reforming data analysis methods in behavioral research. *American Journal of Psychiatry,* 162(3), 643–a–644.

Kline, R. B. (2015). *Principles and practice of structural equation modeling.* Guilford publications.

Kock, N. (2013). Using WarpPLS in e-collaboration studies: Descriptive statistics, settings, and key analysis results. *Interdisciplinary Applications of Electronic Collaboration Approaches and Technologies,* 62–78.

Kock, N. (2014). Advanced mediating effects tests, multi-group analyses, and measurement model assessments in PLS-based SEM. *International Journal of e-Collaboration,* 10(1), 1–13.

Kock, N. (2015a). Common method bias in PLS-SEM: A full collinearity assessment approach. *International Journal of e-Collaboration,* 11(4), 1–10.

Kock, N. (2015b). How likely is Simpson's paradox in path models? *International Journal of e-Collaboration,* 11(1), 1–7.

Kock, N. (2015c). Wheat flour versus rice consumption and vascular diseases: Evidence from the China Study II data. *Cliodynamics,* 6(2).

Kock, N. (2016). Non-normality propagation among latent variables and indicators in PLS-SEM simulations. *Journal of Modern Applied Statistical Methods,* 15(1), 16.

Kock, N. (2017a). WarpPLS User Manual: Version 6.0. Laredo, TX: Script Warp Systems.

Kock, N. (2017b). Which is the best way to measure job performance: Self-perceptions or official supervisor evaluations? *International Journal of e-Collaboration,* 13(2), 1–9.

Kock, N., & Gaskins, L. (2016). Simpson's paradox, moderation, and the emergence of quadratic relationships in path models: An information systems illustration. *International Journal of Applied Nonlinear Science, 2*(3), 200–234.

Kock, N., & Lynn, G. (2012). Lateral collinearity and misleading results in variance-based SEM: An illustration and recommendations. *Journal of the Association for Information Systems, 13*(7).

Kohli, C., Suri, R., & Kapoor, A. (2015). Will social media kill branding? *Business Horizons, 58*(1), 35–44.

Koirala, M., & Charoensukmongkol, P. (2018). Perceptions of bank employees towards corporate social responsibility and work attitudes: A comparison between Nepal and Thailand. *The Sankalpa: International Journal of Management Decisions, 4*(1), 1–24.

Kotur, B. R., & Anbazhagan, S. (2014). Education and work-experience-influence on the performance. *Journal of Business and Management, 16*(5), 104–110.

Kwak, H., Anderson, R. E., Leigh, T. W., & Bonifield, S. D. (2019). Impact of salesperson macro-adaptive selling strategy on job performance and satisfaction. *Journal of Business Research, 94*, 42–55.

Labov, W. (1973). The boundaries of words and their meanings. *New ways of analyzing variation in English*. Washington Georgetown University Press.

Lacoste, S. (2016). Perspectives on social media ant its use by key account managers. *Industrial Marketing Management, 54*, 33–43.

Lamont, L. M., & Lundstrom, W. J. (1977). Identifying successful industrial salesmen by personality and personal characteristics. *Journal of marketing Research, 14*(4), 517–529.

Landau, J. C., & Werbel, J. D. (1995). Sales productivity of insurance agents during the first six months of employment: Differences between older and younger new hires. *Journal of Personal Selling & Sales Management,* 15(4), 33–43.

Le, H., Jiang, Z., & Nielsen, I. (2018). Cognitive cultural intelligence and life satisfaction of migrant workers: The roles of career engagement and social injustice. *Social Indicators Research,* 139(1), 237–257.

Lee, D., & Ganesh, G. (1999). Effects of partitioned country image in the context of brand image and familiarity: A categorization theory perspective. *International Marketing Review,* 16(1), 18–41.

Lee, L. Y., & Sukoco, B. M. (2010). The effects of cultural intelligence on expatriate performance: The moderating effects of international experience. *The International Journal of Human Resource Management,* 21(7), 963–981.

Lee, L. Y., Veasna, S., & Wu, W. Y. (2013). The effects of social support and transformational leadership on expatriate adjustment and performance: The moderating roles of socialization experience and cultural intelligence. *Career Development International,* 18(4), 377–415.

Lee, L., Petter, S., Fayard, D., & Robinson, S. (2011). On the use of partial least squares path modeling in accounting research. *International Journal of Accounting Information Systems,* 12(4), 305–328.

Leeflang, P. S. H., Verhoef, P. C., Dahlström, P., & Freundt, T. (2014). Challenges and solutions for marketing in a digital era. *European Management Journal,* 32(1), 1–12.

Leong, S. M., Busch, P. S., & John, D. R. (1989). Knowledge bases and salesperson effectiveness: A script-theoretic analysis. *Journal of marketing Research,* 26(2), 164–178.

Levin, M. A., Hansen, J. M., & Laverie, D. A. (2012). Toward understanding new sales employees' participation in marketing-related technology: Motivation, voluntariness, and past performance. *Journal of Personal Selling & Sales Management,* 32(3), 379-393.

Levy, M., & Sharma, A. (1993). Relationships among measures of retail salesperson performance. *Journal of the Academy of Marketing Science,* 21(3), 231-238.

Levy, M., & Sharma, A. (1994). Adaptive selling: The role of gender, age, sales experience, and education. *Journal of Business Research,* 31(1), 39-47.

Lieberman, D. A., & Gamst, G. (2015). Intercultural communication competence revisited: Linking the intercultural and multicultural fields. *International Journal of Intercultural Relations,* 48, 17-19.

Limbu, Y. B., Jayachandran, C., Babin, B. J., & Peterson, R. T. (2016). Empathy, nonverbal immediacy, and salesperson performance: The mediating role of adaptive selling behavior. *Journal of Business & Industrial Marketing,* 31(5), 654-667.

Lin, Y. C., Chen, A. S. Y., & Song, Y. C. (2012). Does your intelligence help to survive in a foreign jungle? The effects of cultural intelligence and emotional intelligence on cross-cultural adjustment. *International Journal of Intercultural Relations,* 36(4), 541-552.

Lindell, M. K., & Whitney, D. J. (2001). Accounting for common method variance in cross-sectional research designs. *Journal of Applied Psychology,* 86(1), 114.

Liu, H., Chu, H., Huang, Q., & Chen, X. (2016). Enhancing the flow experience of consumers in China through interpersonal interaction in social commerce. *Computers in Human Behavior,* 58, 306-314.

Loken, B., Barsalou, L. W., & Joiner, C. (2008). Categorization theory and research in consumer psychology. *Handbook of consumer psychology*, 133–165.

Lord, R. G., Foti, R. J., & De Vader, C. L. (1984). A test of leadership categorization theory: Internal structure, information processing, and leadership perceptions. *Organizational Behavior and Human Performance,* 34(3), 343–378.

Lord, R. G., Foti, R. J., & Phillips, J. S. (1982). A theory of leadership categorization. In Hunt J. G., Sekaran, U. & Schriesheim, C. (eds.) *Leadership: Beyond Establishment Views*. Carbondak: SIU Press. 104–121.

MacKenzie, S. B., Podsakoff, P. M., & Fetter, R. (1993). The impact of organizational citizenship behavior on evaluations of salesperson performance. *Journal of Marketing*, 57(1): 70–80.

Madhani, P. M. (2015). Managing salesforce performance: Behavior versus outcome measures. *Compensation & Benefits Review,* 47(2), 81–90.

Malek, M. A., & Budhwar, P. (2013). Cultural intelligence as a predictor of expatriate adjustment and performance in Malaysia. *Journal of World Business,* 48(2), 222–231.

Mangold, W. G., & Faulds, D. J. (2009). Social media: The new hybrid element of the promotion mix. *Business Horizons,* 52(4), 357–365.

Mann, W. R. (2000). *The discovery of things: Aristotle's Categories and their context*. Princeton University Press.

Marshall, G. W., Moncrief, W. C., Rudd, J. M., & Lee, N. (2012). Revolution in sales: The impact of social media and related technology on the selling environment. *Journal of Personal Selling & Sales Management,* 32(3), 349–363.

Mathews, S., Healy, M., & Wickramasekera, R. (2012). The internetalisation of information, knowledge, and interaction components of the firm's internationalisation process. *Journal of Marketing Management,* 28(5–6), 733–754.

Matsumoto, D., & Hwang, H. C. (2013). Assessing cross-cultural competence: A review of available tests. *Journal of Cross-Cultural Psychology,* 44(6), 849–873.

McDaniel, M. A., Schmidt, F. L., & Hunter, J. E. (1988). Job experience correlates of job performance. *Journal of Applied Psychology,* 73(2), 327.

McNeilly, K., & Goldsmith, R. E. (1991). The moderating effects of gender and performance on job satisfaction and intentions to leave in the sales force. *Journal of Business Research,* 22(3), 219–232.

Meadows, K. A. (2003). So you want to do research? 5: Questionnaire design. *British Journal of Community Nursing,* 8(12), 562–570.

Miao, C. F., & Evans, K. R. (2013). The interactive effects of sales control systems on salesperson performance: A job demands–resources perspective. *Journal of the Academy of Marketing Science,* 41, 73–90.

Michaelidou, N., Siamagka, N. T., & Christodoulides, G. (2011). Usage, barriers and measurement of social media marketing: An exploratory investigation of small and medium B2B brands. *Industrial Marketing Management,* 40(7), 1153–1159.

Mintu-Wimsatt, A., & Gassenheimer, J. B. (2004). The problem solving approach of international salespeople: The experience effect. *Journal of Personal Selling & Sales Management,* 24(1), 19–25.

Monat, J. P. (2011). Industrial sales lead conversion modeling. *Marketing Intelligence & Planning,* 29(2), 178–194.

Moncrief, W. C., Babakus, E., Cravens, D. W., & Johnston, M. W. (2000). Examining gender differences in field sales organizations. *Journal of Business Research,* 49(3), 245–257.

Moncrief, W. C., & Marshall, G. W. (2005). The evolution of the seven steps of selling. *Industrial Marketing Management,* 34(1), 13–22.

Moncrief, W. C., Marshall, G. W., & Rudd, J. M. (2015). Social media and related technology: Drivers of change in managing the contemporary sales force. *Business Horizons,* 58(1), 45–55.

Moon, T. (2010). Organizational cultural intelligence: Dynamic capability perspective. *Group & Organization Management,* 35(4), 456–493.

Moore, J. N., Hopkins, C. D., & Raymond, M. A. (2013). Utilization of relationship-oriented social media in the selling process: A comparison of consumer (B2C) and industrial (B2B) salespeople. *Journal of Internet Commerce,* 12(1), 48–75.

Moore, J. N., Raymond, M. A., & Hopkins, C. D. (2015). Social selling: A comparison of social media usage across process stage, markets, and sales job functions. *Journal of Marketing Theory and Practice,* 23(1), 1–20.

Mor, S., Morris, M. W., & Joh, J. (2013). Identifying and training adaptive cross-cultural management skills: The crucial role of cultural metacognition. *Academy of Management Learning & Education,* 12(3), 453–475.

United Nations. (2019). The Sustainable Development Goals Report 2019. https://www.un.org/sustainabledevelopment/gender-equality/

Nelson-Field, K., & Taylor, J. (2012). *Facebook fans: A fan for life?* (Doctoral dissertation, Warc)

Ng, K. Y., Van Dyne, L., & Ang, S. (2009). From experience to experiential learning:

Cultural intelligence as a learning capability for global leader development. *Academy of Management Learning & Education,* 8(4), 511–526.

Nguyen, B., Yu, X., Melewar, T. C., & Chen, J. (2015). Brand innovation and social media: Knowledge acquisition from social media, market orientation, and the moderating role of social media strategic capability. *Industrial Marketing Management,* 51, 11–25.

Nguyen, H., Ashkanasy, N. M., Parker, S. L., & Li, Y. (2018). The role of implicit leadership theory in employees' perceptions of abusive supervision. In *Individual, Relational, and Contextual Dynamics of Emotions* (Vol. 44, pp. 119–138). Emerald Publishing Limited.

Nongpong, S., & Charoensukmongkol, P. (2016). I don't care much as long as I am also on Facebook: Impacts of social media use of both partners on romantic relationship problems. *The Family Journal,* 24(4), 351–358.

Nowlin, E. L., Walker, D., & Anaza, N. A. (2018). How does salesperson connectedness impact performance? It depends upon the level of internal volatility. *Industrial Marketing Management,* 68, 106–113.

Nunan, D., Sibai, O., Schivinski, B., & Christodoulides, G. (2018). Reflections on "social media: Influencing customer satisfaction in B2B sales" and a research agenda. *Industrial Marketing Management.*

Oakes, P. J., Haslam, S. A., & Turner, J. C. (1994). *Stereotyping and Social Reality*: Blackwell Publishing.

Offermann, L. R., & Coats, M. R. (2018). Implicit theories of leadership: Stability and change over two decades. *The Leadership Quarterly,* 29(4), 513–522.

Ogilvie, J., Agnihotri, R., Rapp, A., & Trainor, K. (2018). Social media technology use and salesperson performance: A two study examination of the role of salesperson behaviors, characteristics, and training. *Industrial Marketing Management*, 75, 55–65.

Ogink, T., & Dong, J. Q. (2017). Stimulating innovation by user feedback on social media: The case of an online user innovation community. *Technological Forecasting and Social Change*, 144, 295–302.

Okazaki, S., & Taylor, C. R. (2013). Social media and international advertising: Theoretical challenges and future directions. *International Marketing Review*, 30(1), 56–71.

Oliver, R. L., & Anderson, E. (1994). An empirical test of the consequences of behavior- and outcome-based sales control systems. *Journal of Marketing*, 58(4), 53–67.

Ollier-Malaterre, A., Rothbard, N. P., & Berg, J. M. (2013). When worlds collide in cyberspace: How boundary work in online social networks impacts professional relationships. *Academy of Management Review*, 38(4), 645–669.

Oolders, T., Chernyshenko, O. S., & Stark, S. (2008). Cultural intelligence as a mediator of relationships between openness to experience and adaptive performance. *Handbook of Cultural Intelligence: Theory, Measurement, and Applications*, 145–158.

Ott, D. L., & Michailova, S. (2018). Cultural intelligence: A review and new research avenues. *International Journal of Management Reviews*, 20(1), 99–119.

Ou, C. X., Pavlou, P. A., & Davison, R. M. (2014). Swift guanxi in online marketplaces: The role of computer-mediated communication technologies. *MIS Quarterly*, 38(1), 209–230.

Palmer, A., & Bejou, D. (1995). The effects of gender on the development of relationships between clients and financial advisers. *International Journal of Bank*

Marketing, 13(3), 18–27.

Panagopoulos, N. G., & Avlonitis, G. J. (2010). Performance implications of sales strategy: The moderating effects of leadership and environment. *International Journal of Research in Marketing,* 27(1), 46–57.

Pandey, A., & Charoensukmongkol, P. (2019). Contribution of cultural intelligence to adaptive selling and customer-oriented selling of salespeople at international trade shows: Does cultural similarity matter? *Journal of Asia Business Studies,* 13(1), 79–96.

Park, J. E., & Holloway, B. B. (2003). Adaptive selling behavior revisited: An empirical examination of learning orientation, sales performance, and job satisfaction. *Journal of Personal Selling & Sales Management,* 23(3), 239–251.

Patino, A., Pitta, D. A., & Quinones, R. (2012). Social media's emerging importance in market research. *Journal of Consumer Marketing,* 29(3), 233–237.

Pechmann, C., & Knight, S. J. (2002). An experimental investigation of the joint effects of advertising and peers on adolescents' beliefs and intentions about cigarette consumption. *Journal of Consumer Research,* 29(1), 5–19.

Peng, D. X., & Lai, F. (2012). Using partial least squares in operations management research: A practical guideline and summary of past research. *Journal of Operations Management,* 30(6), 467–480.

Peppers, D., & Rogers, M. (2016). *Managing customer experience and relationships: A strategic framework.* John Wiley & Sons.

Persaud, A. (2005). Enhancing synergistic innovative capability in multinational corporations: An empirical investigation. *Journal of product innovation management,* 22(5), 412–429.

Pettijohn, C. E., Pettijohn, L. S., Keillor, B. D., & Taylor, A. (2000). Adaptive selling and sales performance: An empirical examination. *Journal of Applied Business Research,* 16(1), 91–111.

Pettijohn, C. E., Pettijohn, L. S., & Taylor, A. J. (2007). Does salesperson perception of the importance of sales skills improve sales performance, customer orientation, job satisfaction, and organizational commitment, and reduce turnover? *Journal of Personal Selling & Sales Management,* 27(1), 75–88.

Pfeffer, J. (1985). Organizational demography: Implications for management. *California Management Review,* 28(1), 67–81.

Phungsoonthorn, T., & Charoensukmongkol, P. (2018). The preventive role of transformational leadership and trust in the leader on employee turnover risk of Myanmar migrant workers in Thailand: The moderating role of salary and job tenure. *Journal of Risk Management and Insurance,* 22(2), 66–82.

Piercy, N. F., Cravens, D. W., & Lane, N. (2012). Sales manager behavior-based control and salesperson performance: The effects of manager control competencies and organizational citizenship behavior. *Journal of Marketing Theory and Practice,* 20(1), 7–22.

Piercy, N. F., Cravens, D. W., & Morgan, N. A. (1998). Salesforce performance and behaviour-based management processes in business-to-business sales organizations. *European Journal of Marketing,* 32(1/2), 79–100.

Podsakoff, P. M., MacKenzie, S. B., Lee, Y., & Podsakoff, N. P. (2003). Common method biases in behavioral research: A critical review of the literature and recommended remedies. *Journal of Applied Psychology,* 88(5), 879.

Podsakoff, P. M., & Organ, D. W. (1986). Self-reports in organizational research: Problems and prospects. *Journal of Management,* 12(4), 531–544.

Popp, B., & Woratschek, H. (2016). Introducing branded communities in sport for building strong brand relations in social media. *Sport Management Review,* 19(2), 183–197.

Porter, S. S., & Inks, L. W. (2000). Cognitive complexity and salesperson adaptability: An exploratory investigation. *Journal of Personal Selling & Sales Management,* 20(1), 15–21.

Porter, S. S., Wiener, J. L., & Frankwick, G. L. (2003). The moderating effect of selling situation on the adaptive selling strategy–selling effectiveness relationship. *Journal of Business Research,* 56(4), 275–281.

Predmore, C. E., & Bonnice, J. G. (1994). Sales success as predicted by a process measure of adaptability. *Journal of Personal Selling & Sales Management,* 14(4), 55–65.

Pride, W., & Ferrell, O. (2008). *Marketing.* Boston: Houghton Mifflin Company.

Puyod, J. V., & Charoensukmongkol, P. (2019a). The contribution of cultural intelligence to the interaction involvement and performance of call center agents in cross-cultural communication: The moderating role of work experience. *Management Research Review*, 42(12), 1400–1422.

Villegas-Puyod, J., & Charoensukmongkol, P. (2019b). Emotional intelligence, interaction involvement, and job performance of call center representatives in the Philippines. *Human Behavior, Development and Society,* 20(2), 20–28.

Quinton, S., & Wilson, D. (2016). Tensions and ties in social media networks: Towards a model of understanding business relationship development and business performance enhancement through the use of LinkedIn. *Industrial Marketing Management,* 54, 15–24.

Rachmawaty, N., Wello, M. B., Akil, M., & Dollah, S. (2018). Do cultural intelligence and language learning strategies influence students' English language proficiency? *Journal of Language Teaching and Research,* 9(3), 655–663.

Putranto, N. A. R., Nuraeni, S., Gustomo, A., & Ghazali, A. (2018). The relationship between cultural intelligence, emotional intelligence, and student performance. *International Journal of Business,* 23(1), 17–25.

Rapp, A., Agnihotri, R., & Baker, T. L. (2011). Conceptualizing salesperson competitive intelligence: An individual-level perspective. *Journal of Personal Selling & Sales Management,* 31(2), 141–155.

Rapp, A., Agnihotri, R., & Forbes, L. P. (2008). The sales force technology–performance chain: The role of adaptive selling and effort. *Journal of Personal Selling & Sales Management,* 28(4), 335–350.

Rapp, A., Ahearne, M., Mathieu, J., & Schillewaert, N. (2006). The impact of knowledge and empowerment on working smart and working hard: The moderating role of experience. *International Journal of Research in Marketing,* 23(3), 279–293.

Rapp, A., Beitelspacher, L. S., Grewal, D., & Hughes, D. E. (2013). Understanding social media effects across seller, retailer, and consumer interactions. *Journal of the Academy of Marketing Science,* 41(5), 547–566.

Remhof, S., Gunkel, M., & Schlägel, C. (2013). Working in the "global village": The influence of cultural intelligence on the intention to work abroad. *German Journal of Human Resource Management,* 27(3), 224–250.

Rice, W. R. (1989). Analyzing tables of statistical tests. *Evolution,* 43(1), 223–225.

Rigdon, E. E., Sarstedt, M., & Ringle, C. M. (2017). On comparing results from CB-SEM and PLS-SEM: Five perspectives and five recommendations. *Marketing:*

ZFP–Journal of Research and Management, 39(3), 4–16.

Robinson Jr., L., Marshall, G. W., Moncrief, W. C., & Lassk, F. G. (2002). Toward a shortened measure of adaptive selling. *Journal of Personal Selling & Sales Management,* 22(2), 111–118.

Robinson Jr., L., Marshall, G. W., & Stamps, M. B. (2005). Sales force use of technology: Antecedents to technology acceptance. *Journal of Business Research,* 58(12), 1623–1631.

Rockstuhl, T., & Ng, K. Y. (2008). The effects of cultural intelligence on interpersonal trust in multicultural teams. *Handbook of Cultural Intelligence: Theory, Measurement, and Applications* (pp. 206–220). Routledge.

Rockstuhl, T., Seiler, S., Ang, S., Van Dyne, L., & Annen, H. (2011). Beyond general intelligence (IQ) and emotional intelligence (EQ): The role of cultural intelligence (CQ) on cross-border leadership effectiveness in a globalized world. *Journal of Social Issues,* 67(4), 825–840.

Rodriguez, M., & Boyer, S. (2018). Developing tomorrow's global sales leader: Adapting to cultural differences utilizing role play. *Journal for Advancement of Marketing Education,* 26.

Rodriguez, M., & Honeycutt Jr., E. D. (2011). Customer relationship management (CRM)'s impact on B to B sales professionals' collaboration and sales performance. *Journal of Business-to-Business Marketing,* 18(4), 335–356.

Rodriguez, M., Peterson, R. M., & Krishnan, V. (2013). Social media's influence on business-to-business sales performance. *Journal of Personal Selling & Sales Management,* 32(3), 365–378.

Rollins, M., Nickell, D., & Wei, J. (2014). Understanding salespeople's learning experiences through blogging: A social learning approach. *Industrial Marketing*

Management, 43(6), 1063–1069.

Román, S., & Iacobucci, D. (2010). Antecedents and consequences of adaptive selling confidence and behavior: A dyadic analysis of salespeople and their customers. *Journal of the Academy of Marketing Science,* 38(3), 363–382.

Román, S., & Rodríguez, R. (2015). The influence of sales force technology use on outcome performance. *Journal of Business & Industrial Marketing,* 30(6), 771–783.

Rosch, E., & Mervis, C. B. (1975). Family resemblances: Studies in the internal structure of categories. *Cognitive Psychology,* 7(4), 573–605.

Rosch, E., Mervis, C. B., Gray, W. D., Johnson, D. M., & Boyes-Braem, P. (1976). Basic objects in natural categories. *Cognitive psychology,* 8(3), 382–439.

Russ, F. A., & McNeilly, K. M. (1995). Links among satisfaction, commitment, and turnover intentions: The moderating effect of experience, gender, and performance. *Journal of Business Research,* 34(1), 57–65.

Salo, J. (2017). Social media research in the industrial marketing field: Review of literature and future research directions. *Industrial Marketing Management,* 66, 115–129.

Sanderson, J., & Hambrick, M. E. (2012). Covering the scandal in 140 characters: A case study of Twitter's role in coverage of the Penn State saga. *International Journal of Sport Communication,* 5(3), 384–402.

Sasatanun, P., & Charoensukmongkol, P. (2016). Antecedents and outcomes associated with social media use in customer relationship management of Thai microenterprises. *International Journal of Technoentrepreneurship,* 3(2), 127–149.

Saunders, M., Lewis, P., & Thornhill, A. (2009). *Research Methods for Business Students.*

Pearson Education.

Sax, L. J., Gilmartin, S. K., & Bryant, A. N. (2003). Assessing response rates and nonresponse bias in web and paper surveys. *Research in Higher Education,* 44(4), 409–432.

Schmidt, F. L., Hunter, J. E., & Outerbridge, A. N. (1986). Impact of job experience and ability on job knowledge, work sample performance, and supervisory ratings of job performance. *Journal of Applied Psychology,* 71(3), 432.

Schultz, R. J., Schwepker Jr., C. H., & Good, D. J. (2012). Social media usage: An investigation of B2B salespeople. *American Journal of Business,* 27(2), 174–194.

Scuotto, V., Del Giudice, M., Della Peruta, M. R., & Tarba, S. (2017). The performance implications of leveraging internal innovation through social media networks: An empirical verification of the smart fashion industry. *Technological Forecasting and Social Change,* 120, 184–194.

Shapiro, J. M., Ozanne, J. L., & Saatcioglu, B. (2008). An interpretive examination of the development of cultural sensitivity in international business. *Journal of International Business Studies,* 39(1), 71–87.

Sharma, A., & Levy, M. (1995). Categorization of customers by retail salespeople. *Journal of Retailing,* 71(1), 71–81.

Sharma, A., Levy, M., & Kumar, A. (2000). Knowledge structures and retail sales performance: An empirical examination. *Journal of Retailing,* 76(1), 53–69.

Sharma, N., & Patterson, P. G. (1999). The impact of communication effectiveness and service quality on relationship commitment in consumer, professional services. *Journal of Services Marketing,* 13(2), 151–170.

Shilbury, D., Quick, S., & Westerbeek, H. (2003). *Strategic sport marketing*. Allen & Unwin.

Shoemaker, M. E., & Johlke, M. C. (2002). An examination of the antecedents of a crucial selling skill: Asking questions. *Journal of Managerial Issues*, 118–131.

Siguaw, J. A., & Honeycutt Jr., E. D. (1995). An examination of gender differences in selling behaviors and job attitudes. *Industrial Marketing Management,* 24(1), 45–52.

Simintiras, A. C., Ifie, K., Watkins, A., & Georgakas, K. (2013). Antecedents of adaptive selling among retail salespeople: A multilevel analysis. *Journal of Retailing and Consumer Services,* 20(4), 419–428.

Singh, R., & Das, G. (2013). The impact of job satisfaction, adaptive selling behaviors and customer orientation on salesperson's performance: Exploring the moderating role of selling experience. *Journal of Business & Industrial Marketing,* 28(7), 554–564.

Singh, S., & Sonnenburg, S. (2012). Brand performances in social media. *Journal of Interactive Marketing,* 26(4), 189–197.

Smith, E. E., Shoben, E. J., & Rips, L. J. (1974). Structure and process in semantic memory: A featural model for semantic decisions. *Psychological Review,* 81(3), 214.

SocialMediaExaminer. (2019). https://www.socialmediaexaminer.com/smmworld/

Sohn, D. (2014). Coping with information in social media: The effects of network structure and knowledge on perception of information value. *Computers in Human Behavior,* 32, 145–151.

Sood, S. C., & Pattinson, H. M. (2012). 21st Century applicability of the interaction model: Does pervasiveness of social media in B2B marketing increase business dependency on the interaction model? *Journal of Customer Behaviour,* 11(2), 117–128.

Sozbilir, F., & Yesil, S. (2016). The impact of cultural intelligence (CQ) on cross-cultural job satisfaction (CCJS) and international related performance (IRP). *Journal of Human Sciences,* 13(1), 2277.

Sperber, A. D. (2004). Translation and validation of study instruments for cross–cultural research. *Gastroenterology,* 126, S124–S128.

Spiro, R. L., & Weitz, B. A. (1990). Adaptive selling: Conceptualization, measurement, and nomological validity. *Journal of Marketing Research,* 27(1), 61–69.

Statista. (2019). *Most famous social network sites 2019 by active users.* https://www.statista.com/statistics/272014/global–social–networks–ranked–by–number–of–users/.

Statista. (2019a). *Leading countries based on number of Facebook users as of April 2019.* https://www.statista.com/statistics/268136/top–15–countries–based–on–number–of–facebook–users/.

Statista. (2019b). *Social Media Statistics & Facts.* https://www.statista.com/topics/1164/social–networks/.

Stelzner, M. (2009). Social *Media Marketing Industry Report: how Marketers are using social media to grow their businesses.* whitepapersource. com.

Sternberg, R. J., & Detterman, D. K. (1986). *What is intelligence? Norwood.* New York: Ablex.

Sujan, H., Sujan, M., & Bettman, J. R. (1988). Knowledge structure differences between more effective and less effective salespeople. *Journal of Marketing Research*, 25(1), 81–86.

Sujan, H., Weitz, B. A., & Kumar, N. (1994). Learning orientation, working smart, and effective selling. *Journal of Marketing*, 58(3), 39–52.

Sujan, H., Weitz, B. A., & Sujan, M. (1988). Increasing sales productivity by getting salespeople to work smarter. *Journal of Personal Selling & Sales Management*, 8(2), 9–19.

Sundaram, S., Schwarz, A., Jones, E., & Chin, W. W. (2007). Technology use on the front line: How information technology enhances individual performance. *Journal of the Academy of Marketing Science*, 35(1), 101–112.

Suthatorn, P., & Charoensukmongkol, P. (2018). Cultural intelligence and airline cabin crews members' anxiety: The mediating roles of intercultural communication competence and service attentiveness. *Journal of Human Resources in Hospitality & Tourism*, 17(4), 423–444.

Svatošová, V. (2012). Social media such as the phenomenon of modern business. *Journal of Marketing Development and Competitiveness*, 6(4), 62–84.

Swan, J. E., & Futrell, C. M. (1978). Men versus women in industrial sales: A performance gap. *Industrial Marketing Management*, 7(6), 369–373.

Swani, K., Brown, B. P., & Milne, G. R. (2014). Should tweets differ for B2B and B2C? An analysis of Fortune 500 companies' Twitter communications. *Industrial Marketing Management*, 43(5), 873–881.

Swani, K., Milne, G. R., Brown, B. P., Assaf, A. G., & Donthu, N. (2017). What messages to post? Evaluating the popularity of social media communications in business versus consumer markets. *Industrial Marketing Management*, 62, 77–87.

Szymanski, D. M. (1988). Determinants of selling effectiveness: The importance of declarative knowledge to the personal selling concept. *The Journal of marketing*, 52(1), 64–77.

Szymanski, D. M., & Churchill Jr., G. A. (1990). Client evaluation cues: A comparison of successful and unsuccessful salespeople. *Journal of Marketing Research*, 27(2), 163–174.

Tanchaitranon, N., & Charoensukmongkol, P. (2016). Effects of global networks and the foreign migrant workforce effects on Thai SMEs' satisfaction with their export performance: The mediating role of international knowledge. *International Journal of Globalisation and Small Business,* 8(3), 251–268.

Tanner Jr., J. F., Ahearne, M., Leigh, T. W., Mason, C. H., & Moncrief, W. C. (2005). CRM in sales-intensive organizations: A review and future directions. *Journal of Personal Selling & Sales Management,* 25(2), 169–180.

Tarsakoo, P., & Charoensukmongkol, P. (2019). Contribution of marketing capability to social media business performance. *ASEAN Journal of Management & Innovation,* 6(1), 75–87.

Tenenhaus, M., Vinzi, V. E., Chatelin, Y. M., & Lauro, C. (2005). PLS path modeling. *Computational Statistics & Data Analysis,* 48(1), 159–205.

Teng, S., Khong, K. W., Chong, A. Y. L., & Lin, B. (2017). Persuasive electronic word-of-mouth messages in social media. *Journal of Computer Information Systems,* 57(1), 76–88.

Thomas, D. C., & Inkson, K. (2004). Cultivating your cultural intelligence. *Security Management,* 48(8), 30–33.

Thomas, D. C., Elron, E., Stahl, G., Ekelund, B. Z., Ravlin, E. C., Cerdin, J. L., ...

Lazarova, M. (2008). Cultural intelligence: Domain and assessment. *International Journal of Cross Cultural Management,* 8(2), 123–143.

Trailer, B., & Dickie, J. (2006). Understanding what your sales manager is up against. *Harvard Business Review,* 84(7–8), 48–55, 187.

Trainor, K. J. (2012). Relating social media technologies to performance: A capabilities-based perspective. *Journal of Personal Selling & Sales Management,* 32(3), 317–331.

Trainor, K. J., Andzulis, J., Rapp, A., & Agnihotri, R. (2014). Social media technology usage and customer relationship performance: A capabilities-based examination of social CRM. *Journal of Business Research,* 67(6), 1201–1208.

Triandis, H. C. (2006). Cultural Intelligence in Organizations. *Group & Organization Management,* 31(1), 20–26.

Van Teijlingen, E. R., & Hundley, V. (2001). The importance of pilot studies. *Social Research Update,* (35), 1–4.

Van Zoonen, W., Verhoeven, J. W. M., & Vliegenthart, R. (2017). Understanding the consequences of public social media use for work. *European Management Journal,* 35(5), 595–605.

Verbeke, W., & Bagozzi, R. P. (2000). Sales call anxiety: Exploring what it means when fear rules a sales encounter. *Journal of Marketing,* 64(3), 88–101.

Verbeke, W., Belschak, F., & Bagozzi, R. P. (2004). The adaptive consequences of pride in personal selling. *Journal of the Academy of Marketing Science,* 32(4), 386–402.

Viio, P., & Grönroos, C. (2016). How buyer–seller relationship orientation affects adaptation of sales processes to the buying process. *Industrial Marketing Management,* 52, 37–46.

Vinzi, V. E., Chin, W. W., Henseler, J., & Wang, H. (2010). *Handbook of partial least squares*. Berlin: Springer.

Viswanathan, M., & Childers, T. L. (1999). Understanding how product attributes influence product categorization: Development and validation of fuzzy set-based measures of gradedness in product categories. *Journal of Marketing Research*, 36(1), 75–94.

Wachner, T., Plouffe, C. R., & Grégoire, Y. (2009). SOCO's impact on individual sales performance: The integration of selling skills as a missing link. *Industrial Marketing Management*, 38(1), 32–44.

Wagner, C. H. (1982). Simpson's paradox in real life. *The American Statistician*, 36(1), 46–48.

Walker Jr., O. C., Churchill Jr., G. A., & Ford, N. M. (1977). Motivation and performance in industrial selling: Present knowledge and needed research. *Journal of Marketing Research*, 14(2), 156–168.

Walker, O. C. J., Churchill, G. A. J., & Ford, N. A. (1979). Where do we go from here? Selected conceptual and empirical issues concerning the motivation and performance of the industrial sales force. In G. Albaum & G. A. Churchill, Jr. (Eds.), *Critical Issues in Sales Management: State-of-Theart and Future Research Needs* (pp. 10–75).

Wang, W. Y. C., Pauleen, D. J., & Zhang, T. (2016). How social media applications affect B2B communication and improve business performance in SMEs. *Industrial Marketing Management*, 54, 4–14.

Wang, X., Yu, C., & Wei, Y. (2012). Social media peer communication and impacts on purchase intentions: A consumer socialization framework. *Journal of interactive marketing*, 26(4), 198–208.

Wang, Y., Hsiao, S. H., Yang, Z., & Hajli, N. (2016). The impact of sellers' social influence on the co-creation of innovation with customers and brand awareness in online communities. *Industrial Marketing Management,* 54, 56–70.

WeChat. (2019). 2018 WeChat Statistics Report. https://support.weixin.qq.com/cgi-bin/mmsupport-bin/getopendays.

Weitz, B. A. (1978). Relationship between salesperson performance and understanding of customer decision making. *Journal of marketing Research*, 15(4), 501–516.

Weitz, B. A. (1981). Effectiveness in sales interactions: a contingency framework. *The Journal of marketing*, 45(1), 85–103.

Weitz, B. A., Sujan, H., & Sujan, M. (1986). Knowledge, motivation, and adaptive behavior: A framework for improving selling effectiveness. *Journal of Marketing*, 50(4), 174–191.

Wittgenstein, L. (1953). *Philosophical Investigations./Philosophische Untersuchungen.* Macmillan.

WTO. (2015). *International Trade Statistics* 2015. https://www.wto.org/english/res_e/statis_e/its2015_e/its15_toc_e.htm.

Yan, H., Wickramasekera, R., & Tan, A. (2018). Exploration of Chinese SMEs' export development: The role of managerial determinants based on an adapted innovation-related internationalization model. *Thunderbird International Business Review,* 60(4), 633–646.

Yeap, J. A., Ramayah, T., & Soto-Acosta, P. (2016). Factors propelling the adoption of m-learning among students in higher education. *Electronic Markets,* 26(4), 323–338.

Yunlu, D. G., Clapp-Smith, R., & Shaffer, M. (2017). Understanding the role of cultural intelligence in individual creativity. *Creativity Research Journal,* 29(3), 236–243.

Zallocco, R., Bolman Pullins, E., & Mallin, M. L. (2009). A re-examination of B2B sales performance. *Journal of Business & Industrial Marketing,* 24(8), 598–610.

Zheng, L., & Zheng, Y. (2014). Online sexual activity in Mainland China: Relationship to sexual sensation seeking and sociosexuality. *Computers in Human Behavior,* 36, 323–329.

Zhou, M., Lei, L., Wang, J., Fan, W., & Wang, A. G. (2014). Social media adoption and corporate disclosure. *Journal of Information Systems,* 29(2), 23–50.

Zhu, Z., Wang, J., Wang, X., & Wan, X. (2016). Exploring factors of user's peer-influence behavior in social media on purchase intention: Evidence from QQ. *Computers in Human Behavior,* 63, 980–987.

BIOGRAPHY

NAME	JIHONG ZHOU
ACADEMIC BACKGROUND	Bachelor's degree in English(Economics and Trade) from China University of Geosciences(Wuhan) in 2003 Master's degree in Applied Linguistics from Central China Normal University, Wuhan, China in 2011
EXPERIENCES	Lecturer at Jingchu University of Technology, Hubei, China from 2004–2017